SUNLIGHT IN THE WINE

Life in a Greek island valley

SUNLIGHT IN THE WINE
Life in a Greek island valley

by

ROBERT LEIGH

Drawings by Pat HERON

τυπωθήτω
GEORGE DARDANOS

First Published 1966

τυπωθήτω - GEORGE DARDANOS
99, Har. Trikoupi str., 114 73 -Athens, Greece
Tel. 38.08.334 & 38.08.903 – Fax 38.43.285
Phototypeseting *P. Kapenis* – Tel.-Fax 33.01.607

ISBN 960-7643-22-4
No ed. 21

*For Marylle
and
Tony*

Felos Beach

Vasamia

Gavrion

Tower of Ayios Petros

Batsi

Paleopolis

Apikia

Stenies

Stavropeda

Menites

Yialyia Beach

Monastery of Panachrantos

Messaria

Hora

Zagora

Vourni

Sinetia

Kochylou

Korthion

N

CHAPTER ONE

*I*T WAS A JUNE MORNING WHEN SOTIRIS CAME TO look at the house for us and the valley was brilliant with bright shaking light on the leaves of the olive trees. The water was running high and fast that year and the rocky stream that leaped and spun at the bottom of our little orchard sounded like excited applause. There was a wind, of course, as there usually is on Andros, which made everything but the cypress trees dance, and the doves had chosen that moment to float back to their ancestral white home.

We had bought draught wine from a village store and stood on the terrace eating olives with it while Sotiris took stock of the view.

The village was a little farther up the valley and the blue dome of the Orthodox church with its little cross was just visible above the branches of a huge walnut tree. Natural spring water gushes out of the mouths of lion head gargoyles below the church's marbled steps and there is a taverna just across the road. There were other white houses to be seen farther up the wooded mountain but the deep fold of the green valley really begins where the stream starts gathering force below the taverna.

From there it falls through lemon trees and oleander bushes towards the next village two miles away. There are small terraced fields of barley for the animals as well as orchards in the valley and several of the stone dovecotes which are all over these islands.

Below our house there is a stone bridge over the stream and I saw Sotiris noting how the neat walls marked the terraces on the high wild hillside above it.

When he turned to us there was pleasure on his face and his damaged eye gleamed as sharply as the other one with genuine appreciation. Sotiris is an architect who is in love with the Cycladic islands and has a passionate admiration for the skill and perseverance with which men have made them habitable.

— I think you may have found paradise here, he said. Let's have a look at what we can do with your house then.

Marylle and I had discovered the house when walking through the steep valley paths a couple of years earlier. It stood at the side of a path where the communal channel, which carries water to the fields and orchards, empties down in a small explosive waterfall. There was little about it, apart from its position near the top of the valley, to fall in love with at first. A plain stone building, it appeared to be on just one level with a long flat roof broken by two tall stone chimneys. It was only when we walked around to the back that we discovered it was built on three levels, including the various subterranean chambers where animals had once been quartered, and had a perfect view of the valley with its swirling doves and butterflies.

It also had its own orchard on three narrow strips of terraced land leading down to where wild fig trees grew at the edges of the stream. I think it crossed both our minds at that moment that nothing would be more delightful than falling asleep to the music of its rushing waters. The trees in the orchard included wild cherry and plum, as well as orange and lemon, and there was enough space between them to plant a modest vegetable garden.

We were living outside Athens at the time but Marylle always spent several weeks every summer on Andros, where the mother's side of her family had settled after fleeing from Turkey a hundred and sixty years earlier. The family had kept a house facing the harbour at Chora, which has been the capital of the island since the Venetians first occupied it some seven hundred years ago. Although this makes it sound grand, the entire island only has a resident population of around eight thousand despite the fact that it is almost twenty five miles long. It is no more than a couple of hours by ferry from the mainland but, because it lacks both classical ruins and exotic summer visitors, isn't the kind of island most tourists get into a lather about.

I had been there only three times with Marylle before our walk through the valley and must confess that I hadn't been entranced by it myself. Although we had met some years earlier in London, it was only the previous summer that we had decided to live together in Greece, and I probably still had metropolitan dust in my socks. At all events, although I could see that it was a green and peaceful island, the people I had met didn't immediately strike me as being full of sunny good humour and, in fact, the whole place seemed to have a listless air about it. It certainly didn't give me the impression that it would do very much for my spirits if we were to finish up spending a lot of time there.

I couldn't have been more wrong of course, and the island was to give me a whole new lease on life in time, together with the sense that I was beginning to learn the true pulse of things once more. I have always been able to find ways of enjoying myself but it was the people we got to know after we had bought the house in the green valley who helped me find true pleasure in living again.

This is getting ahead of myself, however, and all I knew at the time was that I found the island rather boring whereas Marylle loved it with a rare passion. I couldn't understand why she wanted us to buy the house by the stream when we could always stay in Chora, but she explained that this house was for the use of all her family and that it would be nice to have a place to ourselves.

A couple of months later we had bought the house and engaged a local mason to do some preliminary restoration work for us. The man we bought it from was the middle son of a woman who had apparently lived in it all her life until she died at over eighty years of age.

He had lived there himself as a boy when the island was occupied during the Second World War but was married now to a woman from another village and had a house of his own. There was no doubt that he still associated the old stone houses in the valley with the hard life he had known there and was surprised that we wanted to buy it. It was true that some of the people who had grown up in the valley had moved out and came back for only a few weeks every summer. It was a long walk up the paths to the village with its church and café bar, after all, and there were no lamps to light the way until a few years ago.

We knew none of our new neighbours then, although it was obvious that some were small farmers who lived from their land and animals. It turned out that the mason working on the house for us, who was called Andreas, had known many of them at school however, and had a great respect for the way they lived, although I think he was puzzled about why an English city slicker wanted to set up house in the valley.

Andreas was a strong wiry man in his sixties, with a dapper talkative edge to him that contrasted sharply with his workmate Nicholas, who was about as chatty as a tree. Nicholas was the labourer who did most of the heavy work while Andreas slapped his cement around with the dash and authority of the seasoned artist.

It was clear that Nicholas, who was a tremendously loyal and hard-working man, had grown out of his environment with a stubborn resistance to any kind of change, whereas there was a definite verve and mobility about Andreas despite his years. I wasn't surprised to learn that he had earned money as a boy by carrying the suitcases of rich summer visitors from the quayside at Chora up to the town itself. This was in the days when there were few cars on the island and people arrived after an eight-hour boat ride from the port of Piraeus.

It was Andreas who made a number of the suggestions about the house and became almost as involved in its renovation as we were. The house had served two families at one time and, in the process of dismantling the brick partitions and opening up the rooms again to their original dimensions, he built some beautiful stone shelves into the walls. He also tiled the floors with grey paving stones and extended the small terrace at the back of the house out over the rooms on the bottom level where the animals had been kept.

I thought his great triumph was the conversion of the room in which the mule had been kept into a friendly little bathroom for us. There had been a separate entrance for the mule in earlier times and Andreas built this up again with stones so that the front wall of the house was now continuous apart from our front door. I was particularly delighted because the room also had a curved stone fireplace with a sooty wooden lintel above it and I fancied the thought of having a bath with a fire singing to me.

We didn't have the money to have all this work done at once and it was spread over about eighteen months while we popped back and forwards from Athens to see what was being done. I was living on savings while trying to finish a book, but it was clear that Andreas didn't really understand why I appeared to just be loafing around half the time. He was far too courteous to enquire further into this but every once in a while liked to emphasise what he thought was the difference between us by little demonstrations of his own energy and strength.

I made the mistake once of volunteering to carry a carton of heavy tiles down the steps to the house from the road at the top. He didn't say a word when I had to pause every fifty yards or so but smiled at me with triumphant charity as he trotted past with two cartons supported on one sturdy shoulder.

There are nearly one hundred and fifty steps on the steep path and he was waiting for me as I stumbled up the last few when we returned for more tiles.

— How are you getting on with that book you're writing?

— It's coming along.

He nodded as he rubbed one strong gnarled hand across his chin.

— It's not the sort of work that gives you much exercise though.

— I suppose not.

There was a small glint in his eyes now and he leaned against a stone wall before reaching for a cigarette.

— I don't know why you don't leave all this heavy work to Nicholas and me. There's no point in straining yourself when you could be at your typewriter.

I liked Andreas enormously and there is no doubt he would have continued working for us but, when visiting his daughter and grandchild in Athens one week, he was knocked down at some traffic lights by two merry kids on a motor scooter. Of course most people in Greece had little money until recently and are pleased to buy these machines for their children nowadays. Unfortunately, it means that the kids are killing themselves by the dozen on the roads every week because they can't handle their freedom and don't want to know about traffic regulations.

It also means that innocent pedestrians like Andreas are getting damaged with more than ordinary frequency and, although I gather that the kids were contrite enough to help him to the nearest hospital, he finished up with a bad case of concussion. He was in bed for months and, when he finally turned up in Andros again, was clearly still suffering from its sick and giddy effects.

He did come to the house one more time to finish some tiling in the bathroom but could hardly stand upright a lot of the time. It was Nicholas, looking sad and puzzled at the clumsy movements of his old friend, who had to do most of the work.

I was stupid enough to run up one of the flights of steps as we went up to the café bar after they had finished and was mortified when I saw Andreas's face as he laboured after me.

— I can't do that sort of thing now, he said. The accident took more out of me than I thought.

We only saw him a couple of times more after that in Chora, and I gather he lives in Athens nowadays in the same building as his son-in-law and daughter. Although Nicholas still lives on the island, he has retired now that he doesn't have Andreas to boss him around, and the couple of times I've run into him, said that he spends most of his time in his garden now.

There was a period of about nine months after this when nothing further was done to the house but then we were introduced to Sotiris by a friend who was employing him to supervise the restoration of a mansion in Chora. It was about time that we consulted a sympathetic architect before doing anything more on the house anyway, and he couldn't have been more perfect for us. Although he has his offices near Piraeus, Sotiris works mostly in the Cyclades and knows many of the old skilled craftsmen who still live and work on the islands.

He is also salty and argumentative enough to appeal to someone like me who suspects anyone of reasonable years without some bite and intelligence to them.

After a meal, in which we both got as merry as fishermen,

he said he would have a look at the house in the valley the following morning.

———

It was a pleasure to show someone around the house who clearly appreciated how the simplicity of its structure reflected the stubborn lives of the generations who had lived there. There was something almost Dutch in the feeling of a hard plain domesticity achieved within resolute walls and the front door opened directly on to what must have been the main living area. There had been a stone sink against one wall before Andreas had demolished it and a handsome fireplace still contained iron cooking utensils in its charred depths.

There were a couple of smaller rooms behind this space and then, through a deep archway in the thick wall, a much larger room which looked out on to the other side of the valley. This had probably been where the previous owners had gathered for special family occasions or entertaining their neighbours. It had a ceremonial feel to it and the corner cupboard, which we were determined to have restored, had surely contained glasses for raki and the little cups for Greek coffee.

The ceilings in every room had great wooden beams with slabs of grey stone above them to support the roof and Sotiris nodded with satisfaction when he saw them.

— The house has been well built, he said. I should make sure those beams are looked at again though.

He hadn't seen anything yet, however, and both Marylle and I were dying to show him two of the house's most dramatic features. The first was another large room with a dirt floor and fallen roof behind the bathroom which was dominated by an enormous fireplace of blackened stone. This was the size of a small cave and at least ten people could have stood inside and looked up through the massive tapering chimney. The old bread oven was in a primitive room down on the bottom level of the house and, in any event, this giant fireplace would have been far too large for general cooking purposes. We decided finally that it must have been used for smoking the pig at the beginning of every winter and, indeed, the man we had bought the house from later confirmed that this had been the case.

The other feature was housed in an outbuilding down on the bottom level below where the waterfall made its splashy din. A broken wooden door hung from one hinge outside and it was as dark as a grave inside, although, in fact, it had been used to nourish and sustain life. The first time I had pulled open the complaining door a terrified green snake had shivered past my feet and something else had brushed through my hair. It had taken us a minute to get used to the gloom inside the building but then we had seen a large millstone propped at an angle on a round concrete block with a small stone chute in front of it.

When Sotiris followed us inside he stood looking around for a while. There was a wooden cradle hanging from a long pole behind the millstone and a number of implements lying scattered on the cobwebbed window sills.

He picked up a wooden spatula and examined it outside in the sun before making a face and smiling at Marylle.

— There must be more of these mills on the island with all this water around, he said. They were used to grind barley and wheat in the old days.

(We had already been told that the mill had been in use until some time after the war. Later that summer we ran into a man who worked for a Greek shipping company in New York but was back in Andros for his holidays. He had lived in a village near Chora as a boy during the war and could remember riding eight kilometres on a mule to have wheat ground for his family at the mill. Apparently, the old lady had only charged ten per cent of the flour as her fee, whereas other mills elsewhere on the island had asked for more).

After inspecting other rooms where the animals had been

2 ROBERT LEIGH, *Sunlight in the wine*

kept we walked back up to the terrace where Sotiris looked at a long crack in the concrete near the back wall of the house.

— We'll have to do something about that as soon as possible, he said. I'll let you have some thoughts about the house in a few days.

The wind had dropped suddenly and we stood there for a few more moments as the valley settled down around us. Apart from the continuous electric commotion of the cicadas, it was extraordinarily still and peaceful, with only a slight disturbance in the leaves of the plane trees below to our right. I saw a saddled mule waiting obediently up on a path opposite us and a black and white goat kneeling at the edge of a steep bank as it fed on some vegetation below it.

Of course the valley wouldn't be the same in winter but I realised at that moment that Sotiris was right and that the house wasn't that far from paradise.

It was a week later when we drove up to a village at the top of the island for one of the most enjoyable meals I have ever eaten. We had been invited by the woman friend who was renovating the mansion in Chora together with Sotiris and seven marble workers. Apparently Sotiris had some suggestions about the house for us and Dora wanted to take everyone out to eat at a place they wouldn't forget. It was Marylle who suggested Yorgo's café up at Vourkoti where we had been on a couple of other excursions.

The seven marble workers, who came from the island of Tinos, which has been famous for the quality of its marble since antiquity, had been brought by Sotiris to cut and fit the window sills and surrounds in the nineteen twenties' mansion. There are 'marmarades' all over Greece but they are usually big, not to say hefty men, and these were definitely on the small side. Since marble is heavy, they were very strong despite their size, however, and had a vaguely epic quality about them, as though they had just emerged from some legendary underground mines. They also looked as though they had all come from the same giant womb, but, in fact, only five were brothers and the other two just colleagues.

(When we all got to drinking the wine at Yorgo's place later, and they lost the reticence that had temporarily settled on them in front of strangers, they became as cheerful and daring as hobgoblins. There was also a marvellous camaraderie between them and I was reminded of the marble men of Carrara in Patience Gray's unique ragbag of a book called 'Honey from a Weed'. This fascinating collection of anecdotes and recipes includes an eloquent hymn to the spontaneity and comradeship of true anarchism and is one of the best books on cookery as a real human activity ever written).

It was just as well we were going up to Vourkoti for I had a feeling the 'marmarades' would have been almost demure in any other setting. The thing about Yorgo's café is that it really wouldn't be out of place in the Yukon or up in some Hebridean village where the men are not averse to alcohol and song. The village itself is the highest place in the island to which the inhabitants fled when pirates came a-marauding and still has a hurried and slightly desperate feel about it. This is certainly not a description of Yorgo, however, who has a stately mien to him which befits his size, and I noticed the magnificent seven looking at him with respect when we got there.

In those days the road to Vourkoti was just a wide stony track across a landscape which wouldn't have seemed unfamiliar to men wearing space suits. I was told by Marylle that even this was a triumph of modern engineering to most islanders and that she had first visited it as a child by mule along high and windy paths. The mountains are only a few thousand feet high but they are bald and alien at the top and the seven kilometre drive passes along the edge of great plunging ravines.

The village itself lies down below the road and can only be reached by climbing down a fierce cascade of over four hundred steps covered here and there by mud and mule drop-pings. It is at the top of these steps that the long steep fall to the distant shining sea comes into view and the reluctance of the pirates to climb all that way just to rape and pillage begins to make sense.

They might have been tempted if Yorgo's place had been there a couple of centuries ago, however, because they would-n't have got a better 'fourtalia' anywhere else. This is a potato omelette served with mountain sausages and pieces of pre-served pig's fat that Yorgo's wife prepares as though she had been born for the purpose. It has similarities to the 'tortilla espanola' Marylle and I were used to eating in Andalucia but then the Mediterranean always throws up these instances of culinary flotsam. We were once served an apple chutney in the Gulf of Corinth which the pension's Italian owner had learned to make from his boy friend, whose Yorkshire mum had given him the recipe.

There is a story in everyone and Yorgo's is that of the island shepherd who became a property owner in the big city. He roamed the land down by the sea with his flock of sheep for years and became the owner of a good part of it. When peo-ple from the mainland began to look at the island for invest-ment he sold great stretches of rocky hillside with sea views and bought flats in Athens. We went down to look at some of his land once and he showed us the grapes from which he makes his wine and the stone trough in which he treads them. It took ninety minutes to climb back to where we had left the car and Yorgo skipped ahead of us with a heavy sack of grapes slung over his shoulder. Of course he was only sixty five years old then and I dare say would have difficulty with the sack nowadays.

It was his huge moon face which looked up as we came to the bottom of the steps and walked into his café.

— Yassas. Isaste kala?

He is a man of great curiosity and it was only after he had

satisfied himself about every member of the party's provenance that they were introduced to his mother. This remarkable old lady with her blue-spotted headscarf and white pinafore always sits near the restaurant door and beams toothlessly at everyone before they enter.

— Kalispera Kirie. Kalispera.

We trooped in to find one long refectory table already laid and open bottles of Yorgo's wine with twists of paper in them as stoppers waiting for us. The faces of the 'marmarades' lit up in unison when they saw these but there was another treat in store for us first. The moment we sat down Yorgo appeared in the doorway carrying a tray of little glasses and a bottle of raki, which is a powerful sp'rit coaxed from the skins and pips of grapes that have been pressed for wine.

When he returned a few minutes later it was to bring plates of salad and his own cheese made from goats' milk. There followed steaming bowls of spaghetti which had been dipped into goats' butter after draining and served with a rich tomato sauce, platters of roasted goat, and a delicate Greek dish in which the flowers of young courgettes are stuffed with fresh cheese and then immersed in batter before frying.

While we were eating Sotiris explained to Marylle and me that he had decided we didn't really need the services of an architect for the house. He knew a skilled older mason who would know exactly what to do about any structural problems we might encounter. As for himself, he was quite willing to be consulted on design matters, but he liked all Marylle's ideas so far and thought she didn't really need much advice.

Marylle was purring by this time of course, and the 'marmarades' seemed to approve as well. They were grinning animatedly at us as they ate and bottles of wine were disappearing as fast as Yorgo could bring fresh supplies. There was a giant old-fashioned jukebox in a corner of the room behind us and Sotiris got up at one point to look through the records. He put the money in for the titles he wanted and returned to

Yorgo from Vourkoti with his mohter

the table just as Yorgo came in bearing bowls of fruit for us.

I don't remember what the first songs were but it doesn't matter because there is a common family feeling in all Greek music. The most banal love songs still share some of the same stock of pain and yearning that makes modern Greek culture one of the most genuinely popular in the world. This is probably because expressions of national feeling weren't encouraged under Turkish occupation and now everyone wants to sing together. It is a culture in which composers have an extraordinarily wide range and great poets are happy to write lyrics which will be heard in nightclubs and music halls.

The other note that is present in all Greek music is full of the sadness that comes when summer ends, the sea starts turning grey around the islands again, and life slowly darkens towards everyone's old age.

It is a powerful emotional mixture for any Greeks with good red wine inside them and the seven men of Tinos had gone through a number of bottles by this time. I believe it was Sotiris who started the singing but they needed no encouragement and soon the rafters were ringing and the fat jukebox bouncing on the wooden floor.

When Yorgo came in to see what was going on a Mikis Theodorakis song was playing and he started singing along with the rest of us. It was a fetching song about sacrificial mothers and I saw to my astonishment that even the toughest looking little marble worker was on the edge of manly tears.

Of course the relationship between most Greek mothers and their sons is so charged and mysterious that it can almost seem perverse. I have been told about women who continue to take special titbits for their sons to eat even after they are married and living in their new homes. Not long ago I spoke to one wife whose burly new husband was enraged that she didn't feed him with a spoon in the mornings as his mother had done. This extreme devotion to male offspring is partly due to the importance of having a son to support and protect the family in hard times. It probably also has much to do with the fact that many marriages, at least among the wealthier people, were arranged with older men until recently and the emotional frustration this caused in their young wives.

When the jukebox stopped shuddering and the music came to an end Yorgo lifted his enormous plump arms and embraced each one of the seven 'marmarades' in turn.

Sotiris winked at me and Dora grinned at Marylle. The evening had been a great success all around.

After shaking hands with Yorgo we left the café and began the long climb back up the steps to where we had parked the cars. The moon was just a thin gleaming crescent but I had brought a torch with me and marched ahead to light the way. At the top I stopped to count the others past me but we seemed to be missing one of the 'marmarades'. I was debating whether to go back and look for him when he swayed into view still singing the Theodorakis song to himself.

When I looked at him I saw he was the youngest of the five brothers and probably quite used to being left behind.

It was past midnight when we drove back down the mountain and the lights of the small harbour below us were etched into a black and motionless sea. There was a feeling of immense space around us in which people clung to whatever they felt was real and I found myself thinking again about the house in the little green valley.

Although I didn't know it then, I had already started falling in love with the whole idea of living there and was only waiting for the right people to come along and make my imagination come alive again.

This was to happen sooner than I thought and I wound up spending most of my time over the next eighteen months in the company of some remarkable island people, many of whom helped in restoring the house and also shared their lives in some ways with Marylle and me.

CHAPTER TWO

*W*E MET THE NEW MASON SOTIRIS HAD FOUND FOR us a couple of weeks later at the house itself. It was early summer on the island now and he came down the steps from the village wearing denim shorts over gnarled bandy legs and a peaked cap on his head. He could have been anything over fifty and under eighty by the look of him but there was a pushy thrust to his body as he came through the door and a fierce glare to his blue eyes which suggested the former. When I got to know him better he admitted reluctantly that he was coming up to seventy but had never felt fitter in his life. It was also quite obvious that he was as stubborn as a goat and could no more stop working than he could alter the other habits of a lifetime.

When Sotiris introduced him to us it turned out that he was also called Yorgo but was from another village on the sea about fifteen kilometres away. He mumbled something to Marylle and shook my hand before looking around at the inside of the house.

— What needs to be done here then? he asked. Someone's put in a lot of good work already.

After telling him about Andreas, and what had happened to him, Marylle led the way outside and showed him the rest of the house from the terrace.

— There's still a lot to do before it is ready as you can see, she said. We can't afford to pay for everything at once though.

Yorgo moved his strong old shoulders in a kind of recognition as he glanced at the terraced walls across the valley and then looked back at the house.

— Where do you want me to start then?

— I think you'd better tell us. It depends on what it will cost.

Sotiris had been examining the glaring crack in the terrace near the wall of the house and called Yorgo over to look at it.

— What do you think about this?

The old mason looked at it with little apparent interest and said something in a rough quick voice I couldn't follow. When I stared enquiringly at Sotiris he just shrugged and lit another cigarette.

— He says the wall is beginning to walk a little but it will be all right if the crack is cemented over. He also says you should put paving stones on the terrace to help buttress the wall.

It turned out that Yorgo didn't think this was that urgent though and so we went through to look at the large room with the fallen roof and the giant black fireplace. There were the remains of a smaller room behind it with just two and a half walls standing which was perched above the bottom level of the house and looked out over the stream.

We had vaguely thought of taking down the wall between the two rooms and putting in a large picture window at the far end but Sotiris shook his head when he heard this.

— It would make this room far too large. It is best to try and keep the proportions that are already here in the house.

This was obviously true and Marylle frowned as she looked at the broken little room with its jagged walls.

— What can we do with it then?

— It's the perfect space for a bathroom. You'll need another one for guests anyway.

— That means we'd have to put in just an ordinary window.

— Of course. You should still be able to sit in the bath and talk to the trees though.

Marylle made another face as she stared at the only two spaces for windows in the larger room with the fireplace.

— It would make it rather dark and gloomy in here wouldn't it?

Sotiris glanced up at the huge wall dividing the two rooms.

— I don't imagine you'd want a bathroom which is two metres high. It would be simpler to put in a lower roof and then Yorgo could open a new window up there for you.

After a little more talking this was what we decided to do and Yorgo agreed to begin work the following week. We wanted to be there when he started but I was booked for a medical examination in a hospital outside Athens and it was ten days later when we arrived back on the island. Walking down the steps that evening we could see that he had already finished the bathroom walls and put in a concrete roof about four feet below the height of the house.

It was only when we got nearer that we saw there was also a new wooden ceiling above the room with the fireplace and that a great pile of stone chips had been deposited on the path. We rushed to look as soon as we got into the house and discovered that a window frame had been fixed with putty into the bathroom wall with a view of the rioting fig trees around the stream.

There was also another frame above the bathroom door which curved like a huge wooden eye at the top. The arch of stones, which had been cemented into the wall surrounding it, matched precisely the curved and smoky stones above the vast fireplace on the other side of the room.

There was silence as we both gazed up at it solemnly and Marylle was looking puzzled when she turned to me.

— Do you suppose it was Yorgo's idea to have it done like that?

— I don't know.

I had been prowling about trying to work out the view we would have through the arched window from different parts of the room when it was. finished. We had decided to have a refectory table in the room and, from the chair I was sitting at in my mind, I would be able to see the pale branches of a plane tree and a white house up on the other side of the valley between them.

From where Marylle was standing we would look up to see the soft high spikes of a line of cypresses and the glazed sky soaring above them.

I had supposed that Yorgo would be working with just one dour and craggy mate as Andreas had done but when we turned up again the following morning the house was alive with people. It turned out that he normally worked with two assistants but had recruited a couple of local men that day to help with laying a concrete roof over the wooden ceiling in the large room.

One of the men was Nico, who owned three mules and earned money by using them to carry everything from building materials to fodder for the animals around the valley paths. The other was his brother Philippos, who I had last seen working in a field with a cassock tucked around his hips and pieces of barley in his black beard. Although he worked the land like everybody else, he also officiated at a church a few kilometres away, and may have been the most tough and durable priest on the island.

There was a chaos of activity on the roof as we arrived, with stone chips being shovelled into position and Yorgo shouting orders at everyone. There was a drop of about three feet from the edge of the roof to a pile of large flat stones on the path but, when he saw us, he put his weight on one rough hand and swung himself down like a young man.

— Kalos irthate.

It was time for the morning coffee break but we wanted to congratulate him on the beautiful arched window first and Marylle pointed to it immediately we entered the room.

— Whose idea was it to make the window in that shape?

Yorgo pushed the cap farther up on to his balding head and rubbed his chin with a sound like sandpaper on splintered wood.

— Don't you like it then?

— Of course we do. We just wanted to know whether you decided to do it that way.

He shrugged and a look that .was almost guilty crumpled his weathered face.

— It wasn't me. Sotiris said you'd like it done in that style.

We should have realised that Sotiris had thought of it but what was certainly down to Yorgo was the way the arch of stones around the frame had been shaped to draw the eye.

The other men joined us a few minutes later and Marylle made Greek coffee for them on a portable electric stove in little metal jugs. I had brought along some brandy to liven up the coffee and because I wanted the men to talk, but I noticed that Yorgo looked disapproving and refused to take some himself. There was some relaxed laughter and conversation for about twenty minutes but then everyone rose to their feet as Yorgo stood up and went outside to continue working.

It became clear after a while that Yorgo was something of a martinet by nature but exercised his authority largely through the insistent example of his own hard work. Since he was pay-master the others had to follow but I got the distinct impression that they were glad to be caught up in his stubborn driving rhythms anyway. He was the man leading the operation and the others moved to his speed in an intricate and purposeful dance of work. We watched as cement was mixed and carried up to him until he looked at his watch and nodded firmly and everyone filed back into the house again.

The time had arrived for their midday meal and I realised over the next few days that it never varied and that everything was always laid out as carefully as at a festive picnic. The only furniture we had in the house at the time were a couple of small rickety tables we had found there, together with a few strange green chairs with webbed plastic seats. These were set out in the long room with a view of the valley and each man produced a container with the food his wife had given him and a bottle of beer.

Marylle and I had intended to eat something at a taverna but we were offered so many savoury titbits by everyone that we were soon full anyway. A bottle of wine from a mountain village appeared from somebody's bag after a few minutes and the heated conversation that followed was about the merits of wines from different parts of the island.

The meal break lasted exactly thirty minutes and I saw that Yorgo was quite happy to take a back seat as the other men gossiped and smoked their cigarettes.

It was straight back to work after that though and the routine was followed precisely over the next ten days. The men were always at work by eight o'clock in the morning and, apart from coffee and the meal break, worked through without stop until three o'clock in the afternoon. This was in the middle of June with a high and unremitting Aegean sun.

After the first couple of days Nico and his brother the priest weren't required any more and Yorgo worked on with his two formidable assistants. They were both nearly as old as him but were so strong and active that we soon got used to this incredible gang of pensioners toiling away on the house every morning.

The youngest of them was by far the most lively and introduced himself cheerfully as Yianni the seaman. He was the one who had produced the bottle of wine and obviously liked to consider himself a bit of a card. Although I gathered he had worked on Greek merchant ships for over twenty five years, he still had glossy black hair only touched warningly with grey here and there and bright convivial eyes.

He was the one operating the pneumatic drill with great enjoyment on the roof the day after we discovered there were mice above the main bathroom. Apparently this part of the roof had been covered with a thick layer of earth before being cemented some years before and the mice had found their way into it. When I climbed up one day to inspect what he had done he was leaning on the silent drill in the middle of a chaos of rubble.

— Are you sure there are still no mice around? I asked. I thought I heard scratching sounds in the bathroom earlier.

He grinned at me as he lit a cigarette.

— The mice will be in Tinos now.

— What do you mean?

Tapping the drill, he imitated its clattering roar.

— Brrrmm, brrrmm. They run away with the noise of this.

— How do you know they won't come back?

— We put new roof here with no earth beneath. They stay away.

Although the other assistant was clearly older, he seemed to do most of the heavy work, as Nicholas had done with Andreas, and was now shovelling the heavy pieces of broken cement from the roof. He had the same deliberate unhurried movements as Nicholas as well but was taller with a quiet lined face and hands that could have torn a piano apart. Watching him, I saw that a stolid, uninvolved patience was as much part of his character as a workhorse, and asked Yianni how old he was.

— I think he is sixty five.

— What about you?

Yorgo, the seventy year old mason

The same grin beamed out again.

— I'm the baby of the team. I'm sixty early next year.

A couple of days later Yorgo had to drive in to Chora to buy materials and I suggested that Yianni and his mate start building some steps we wanted. Apparently the previous owners had entered the orchard over a stone stile down the path but it seemed much easier to put in steps down to each level from the lower part of the house.

I was amazed at how quickly they did the first flight because they must have used at least one hundred stones of varying shapes and sizes. Fortunately, there was a tumbledown wall only a few yards away they could dismantle but were clearly so used to making instant judgements about the size of the stones required at each stage that they must have built many such steps before. It was Yianni who was in charge of construction of course, and the other man who carried stones and mixed the cement with the same closed and stoical expression on his face all the time.

They completed the other two flights of steps down to the orchard above the stream the next day while Yorgo was working on the house. This time I was baffled by where they had managed to find the stones but then saw that they had unearthed a great pile beneath one of the terraced walls. I realised that the orchard was probably full of them under the soil and wasn't surprised when I thought about it. The entire island seems to be made of a grey fissile stone with a rich top soil washed down from its four mountains into the fertile valleys near the sea.

It was extraordinary to me that two men with almost one hundred and thirty years between them had completed all that heavy work in one day but they obviously considered it quite normal. When I asked Yorgo how long they would carry on working before they retired he just shrugged his shoulders.

— They are still strong, he said. They like to keep active as long as possible anyway.

(A couple of days after this I bumped into an extremely ancient priest walking slowly up a flight of more than three hundred steps. After we got talking he told me that he had to climb those steps every day. It is true that the people of Andros have a reputation for longevity, as an inspection of the tombstones in its cemeteries will confirm, and this is usually attributed to its climate. There is no doubt that its air is bracing to say the least and that the island bubbles everywhere with fresh water springs. It is also a humped and twisting island though, and is full of steep paths, many of which were built centuries ago. I think the priest was right and that the islanders spend so much of their lives climbing these steps that they have no time to get old.)

It was the first week in July when most of the construction work on the main living level of the house was completed. The view coming down the steps from the village now was of a very large flat roof nearly thirty yards long and twelve at its widest point. Of course it wasn't completely regular in height, but with the new water tank and solar panels the plumber had installed, we thought it looked very impressive.

(What we wanted to do later was to have a little wall built around the perimeter and then have the roof itself daubed with whitewash in one of those Greek patterns that look like the design for a honeycomb.)

The room with the huge fireplace and the new little bathroom were finished but we needed the plasterers for the walls before Yorgo could lay the floor tiles. He had work on another house to do in the meantime, and the plasterers couldn't start for three weeks, so we wouldn't see him again for a while.

We sat around the rough old wooden table while he worked out what we owed him with the help of a stubby pencil and some pieces of notepaper covered with thick scribbles.

The figure he arrived at finally was reasonable but we didn't have sufficient in the local bank and funds would have to be transferred from Athens. He watched our faces as we muttered to each other and promptly arrived at the wrong conclusion.

— It doesn't matter if you don't have it now, he said in his rough cheerful voice. I can always lend it to you.

Marylle looked at the old mason in his denim shorts and cap with amazement.

— What do you mean?

— Like I said. You can pay it back to me later when you've got the money.

It was the first time anyone had ever offered to loan us the money to pay for his own work and Marylle smiled as she shook her head.

— That's very nice of you but we have enough. It's just that you'll have to wait a few days for it.

We made arrangements to meet him in his village to pay the money and then talked a little about the kind of flagstones we wanted on the terrace. He had apparently used some he thought we might like at another house in the hills behind his village and we said we would take a look at them.

As we left the waterfall was making its merry din and Yorgo looked at it with approval.

— Nice place you're going to have here, he said. I'll have to come back and see it when it's all finished.

CHAPTER THREE

*T*HE HOUSE WAS COMING ALONG NICELY NOW BUT, OF course, there were still many things to be organised, including the wooden beams in every room with the flat grey stones above them. We had met a man called Antonis the previous year who we were told worked mostly at restoring the interiors of little old churches and was a magician with beams. He had been playing the violin at a village festival when we spoke to him and we were so impressed by his talents that we were determined he should do the work for us. Unfortunately, he fell ill shortly after this and it had taken all this time before he agreed to work his wizardry on our forlorn and grimy old beams.

As it happened, he was the brother of one of our neighbours and lived at the top of the valley, so we gave him a door key and left him to it. This was convenient for us anyway since the carpenter had to make some measurements and Antonis could let him into the house for us.

The following week we drove over the mountain to see Yorgo at his village. He had told us where we could inspect the terrace with the flagstones he had laid earlier that year and we decided he must have meant a house high up on the mountain slope above the rich green Korthi valley. There was a man tending the water supply in his swamp of a new garden and he was happy for us to look around the place.

We didn't think the terrace was that attractive but the owner insisted on showing us the rest of his property with such pride that we couldn't refuse. He was clearly a local man who had made money elsewhere in the world and returned to build a house with the kind of views that made it obvious how wealthy he had become. The island architecture is very distinctive but he had resisted its charms and built himself a large modern box with huge windows.

He was hurt when we refused coffee but we wanted to see an exhibition of marble artefacts before the meeting with Yorgo and were in a hurry. It was about five minutes later when we passed another house with a terrace of raised grey stones which almost glowed in the late afternoon sun.

— That must be the place, I said. We've just got enough time to have a look if we hurry.

Marylle shook her head firmly.

— I'd feel embarrassed after our last experience, she said. Let's just drive on.

We didn't buy any of the marble exhibits but everyone seemed to know where Yorgo lived and we parked the car to walk through the village. He was working in his spacious garden when we got there and we were presented with a large bagful of apples before being taken to meet his wife. It wasn't surprising to find that she was a pleasant muted grey-haired lady who spent her time bringing us a series of sweet morsels from her very productive kitchen.

There seemed to be no limit to Yorgo's appetite for work but when I asked him how much sleep he got he said he usually went to bed just before midnight although also slept an hour every afternoon.

— Where do you get your energy from then?

It was a question which obviously embarrassed him and he muttered something about eating a lot of fish and not smoking before taking us to the flat roof of his two-storeyed house. He pointed out some of the houses up in the hills he had built and I noticed that there seemed to be a number of derelict old dovecotes around as well. When we went back downstairs there were pears on the table for us to take away and we left Yorgo tramping determinedly back into his garden.

As we drove back I was thinking about dovecotes and of the people like Yorgo who built them and helped give Andros a slightly abrasive and defiant character of its own.

The island is known primarily today for its shipowners who include some of the most famous and wealthy shipping families in the world. There is scarcely a family today which didn't have at least one male member away at sea until recently and one handsome village is populated almost entirely by sea captains. It is said that Andros hasn't encouraged tourism because shipping has made it wealthy anyway but it is more likely that men away at sea didn't want strangers near their families.

This reputation of a largely maritime island is of only recent origin though as a drive through most parts of it will confirm. The most obvious feature of it is the number of curious stone walls which divide the island up into many thousand fields. It becomes clear at once that at one time the population was composed largely of farmers who cultivated the fertile land in the valleys and kept livestock behind those fascinating walls. A walk into any green part of the island will also reveal the main reason why it must have been a farming paradise in the past and no doubt could easily become so again.

I don't suppose any island which isn't tropical gives the impression that life has ever been easy for its inhabitants but Andros has one natural advantage over many in the Aegean. It has enough fresh water of its own to grow virtually anything in the healthy soil lying in its valleys. The island certainly doesn't get more than its share of rain and the theory is that the water probably originates in the high mountains in its huge neighbouring island of Euboea and is then thought to make its way through mysterious runnels under the sea bed before bubbling up again as dozens of lively and beautiful springs.

Whether this is true or not, fresh water runs freely throughout the year in many parts of the island, and one of its most successful commercial products is a brand of mineral water sold all over Greece.

Evidence for exactly how the islanders lived in past centuries is a little thin on the ground but there is no doubt that they cultivated the land extensively. An English clergyman who visited the Cyclades in the late 1870s and produced a classic book about them,[1] wrote that much of Andros was a vast lemon grove, with boxes of them being sent regularly to England. Since the British Admiralty had adopted the practice of providing every man at sea with an ounce of lemon juice a day to wipe out scurvy only a half century earlier the yellow fruit was probably in great demand at the time.

The formidable cleric also wrote that corn grew in abundance on the island, that it had won a medal of the first class for agriculture at the Paris Exhibition of 1867, and that, in his view, almost anything the islanders chose to grow would prosper with sensible management.

For centuries before this Andros had also been famous for its silk production, which seemed to have persisted on this green island for longer than elsewhere in Greece. It appears that two Persian monks smuggled the first silk worm eggs into the Byzantine Empire in the sixth century and by mediaeval times Greek silk was known all over Europe. According to Lawrence Durrell, in his heated but fascinating book ' The Greek Islands', the Andros weave was celebrated as far afield as Avignon, where, I seem to remember reading

---

1. «The Cyclades: or Life Among the Insular Greeks.» J.T.Bent.

somewhere, the fashion in bodices had become very revealing.

James Bent writes that the silk trade continued to prosper in Andros until the early years of the nineteenth century, when a severe disease affected the hitherto productive and obliging silk worms. It was in a desperate attempt to renew their fortunes, apparently, that the islanders cut down most of the mulberry trees on which the worms had fed and planted even more lemon trees in their place.

(Bent records that island women who wanted to ensure a healthy crop of silk would appear naked on the flat roofs of their houses at dawn on a May morning. This was allegedly to encourage the silk worms but I have yet to find anyone today who seems prepared to believe this really happened.)

It seems clear that Andros was a fairly wealthy agricultural island until just over one hundred and thirty years ago and then a blight on her famed lemon trees led to a number of people having to seek their fortunes elsewhere. These were the years when islanders started emigrating to America leaving their plots of land to wither and dry through lack of care. This gradual abandonment of much of the land continued this century as many people moved to the mainland after the Second World War in search of apparently more exciting economic opportunities.

The result of this process today is that the island has lost much of its former agrarian glory and the little that is produced in its fields and orchards now is just for local consumption. Of course, it is still a comparatively wealthy island compared to many but owes this now to the shipping industry and not to agriculture. There is no reason why it shouldn't be farmed successfully again, however, as far as I can see, if people are prepared to work the land back to its original condition.

(As I write this, I see that some land not far from this valley is being seriously cultivated with a view, I take it, to selling the produce commercially, since a large stretch is involved. A local shipowner has also established a busy vineyard not far away and the sight of a number of women bent over picking his grapes recently was nicely reminiscent of the more prosperous French countryside.)

The only visible evidence of the island's busy agricultural past nowadays are the walled fields and I was thinking about these as we drove back from Yorgo's house. There was a connection in my mind because it is impossible to drive past this stone network of walls without becoming aware of the extraordinary amount of sheer hard work that went into them. I imagined legions of silent dogged men carrying enormous quantities of stones as the old mason's ancestors barked their rough commands.

Although James Bent didn't find the walls picturesque, they have a definite fascination of their own which strikes everyone new to the island. This is because of the unique way they are constructed, with great flat stones positioned vertically every yard or so between smaller stones placed on top of each other in the normal fashion. The perfectly sensible reason for this was to reduce the number of stones used, and I can't think why the technique isn't used more widely, but the impression is of something done for crude magical effect. There is something very primitive and insistent about them, as though they had been erected for mysterious ritual purposes by neolithic men.

The sheer number of fields bounded by these walls points to a large population of farmers with their separate plots of land, although there were, and still are, larger estates owned by wealthier people. Many of these trace their ancestry back to Venetian families who began to settle on the island in the thirteenth century after feudal lords of the Fourth Crusade had attacked and occupied Constantinople in 1204.

It was the first time that the great Byzantine city had been conquered since Constantine had fixed the capital of the Roman Empire there in the early fourth century. There is still controversy over why the crusaders, who were supposed to be on their way to Jerusalem, assaulted a Christian city instead, but it was almost certainly down to the Venetians, who provided the ships and saw Constantinople as a commercial rival. In any event, the result was that the Byzantine Empire was carved up by a bunch of thugs, with the nephew of the Venetian doge eventually founding a state in the Cycladic Islands.

The families who moved down from the Venetian marshes into Andros built large square towers on their estates from which to pour boiling oil on pirates. I have also read that they were given landowners' rights to maintain handsome dovecotes on their lands at the same time, but a local scholar tells me there is no evidence for this at all. It is true that another book on Tinos, the neighbouring island, says that similar dovecotes there weren't built until three hundred years later. I prefer the idea that the Venetians did, in fact, have them built to remind them of the beautiful wheeling birds in their home city, but I suppose nobody will ever really know.

Whatever their origins, these dovecotes were to remain a singular feature of the island from then on. The local peasants had to work the land for successive land owners, of course, and were also obliged, it seems, to maintain the dovecotes, which can be as large as small houses, even though the doves were a constant source of damage to their crops. It may have been resentment about this which caused farmers to start killing them in the late nineteenth century when most of the estate owners had gone into business on the mainland or abroad.

By this time they presumably thought of them as edible vermin, for tiny roast doves were popular at the turn of the century and birds were also pickled in oil and vinegar to be sold in other countries. There was a temporary increase in the number of dovecotes on the island at this time, as the local hunters realised the profit in the birds and built more, but, many of them have gone to wrack as well as ruin since then. Not unexpectedly, the number of birds declined at the same time

The doovecote on th eother side of our stream

although today it seems to me that they are drifting back to their ancestral homes once more.

These were the thoughts in my head as we drove over the warm mountain that evening and the following Saturday afternoon I took a closer look at the dovecote across the stream from our house. The strange thing is that some of the dovecotes on the island are almost works of art in their own right, with elegant fretted little windows and minuscule towers at each corner, but this one is almost plain. Although it is draped with ivy it is definitely an inferior structure but is nonetheless tenanted by a large number of birds who clearly feel attached to it.

It was a quiet still afternoon as I waited on the terrace for the head plasterer who was coming to inspect the amount of work his men would have to do in a couple of weeks time. There were a couple of hawks circling lazily above the fields and a line of about thirty birds perched on the dovecote watching them. It was the first time I had really studied them, and I noticed that there were marginally more pigeons than doves, although they looked quite contented sitting there together.

There was another dovecote a little further down the valley which looked more luxurious to me and I was puzzled as to why the one opposite was more popular. I walked over to satisfy my curiosity while the plasterer was making his calculations and saw the reason at once. The dovecote belonged to the elderly couple in the house below us and, after I had walked up the steep path behind the house, noticed a rocky outcrop about fifteen metres high set into the hillside above it. This was protected by its position from the prevailing wind and, just as importantly, was ridged with a number of natural ledges. The doves had flown away from the dovecote at my approach and, after curling out in a long sweep above the rustling trees, drifted back to settle on these ledges and await my departure. I didn't know whether there was any pecking order involved in the positions they took but it seemed to me that the grey fatter pigeons had commandeered the higher ledges for themselves.

I had seen other dovecotes on the island with no feathered inhabitants but which had been kept in near pristine condition for decorative reasons. This one was dirty and flaking but had as many signs of life as a tenement in a crowded city. There was a kind of covered cellar at the bottom for stabling mules and stacks of hay inside the main building below a series of broad niches where the birds nested. In the field beside it a goat was nibbling away at dried grasses and great quinces with powdery skins hung from a tree by the path.

As I walked back I stopped beside a pool formed in a deep hollow by water which trickled down mysteriously from dark green rocks. There was a gnarled plane tree standing like an old boxer by the side of the water and the pool itself had been shaped by a wall of stones built to support the terrace of lemon trees above it. I was struck again by the incredible amount of hard work that had gone into the cultivation of the island and thought of stubborn old men in previous centuries crouching there in the green hollow as they heaved the wall into existence.

I had forgotten how much secret places with water can refresh the heart and I was remembering a pond I had loved as a small boy when I heard the plasterer yelling for me. When I got back I found him looking inside the mill and he told me afterwards that an 'archon' must have owned the house in the past. An 'archon' means a lord or aristocrat but there were a number of water mills in the valley last century and I do not see how all the owners could have had positions of authority.

Before I walked back up to the village with the plasterer I pointed out a narrow aperture about twenty inches high in the side of the wall of the house. It went back only about a foot into the wall but had clearly been there to look through in past times and had been blocked up when the giant fireplace had been built. Marylle didn't want it covered over with plaster and the man nodded in immediate understanding when I told him.

— I've seen slots in the wall in old houses like this before, he said. They were there for the inhabitants to see when the Turks were coming. I wouldn't fill it in myself.

I've no idea whether he was right or not but, if he was, it meant that the house was over two hundred years old at the very least, since the last Turkish governor of the island departed early in the nineteenth century.

After he had driven away I walked to the café bar where I liked to drink and listen to the villagers talking. It had been rented for most of the summer by a friendly but worried little man with two daughters called Dimitri who had previously worked in New York. Strangely enough, I had run into him earlier that year in a pizza restaurant near Athens. I gathered from his conversation with one of the waiters that he had been employed there as a chef but was leaving that day to run a place in the village where he had been born. When I realised he was talking about the village in Andros where we were restoring the house I introduced myself and promised to be a regular client.

The village is a small community and the only way for him to attract enough trade out of season would have been to offer something different to the other café bars in that part of the island. He agreed with me when we talked about this but by the end of the summer the only customers he had left were a few stalwarts sipping beer. There certainly wasn't enough regular custom for him to support a family and he was looking more morose than usual as he served me my ouzo with small chunks of stewed octopus and bread.

When I asked him whether he would be staying open during the winter months he shrugged and beckoned a small boy on a tricycle across to him. The boy had dirty knees and the kind of determined little face that often causes old ladies to back away in alarm.

Dimitri glanced at me tiredly after giving the boy an ice cream and rubbing his head with rough affection.

— This village will not keep that one when he grows up, he said. He will become a sailor and travel the world.

He seemed a little bleak as he watched the boy pedal away furiously towards the walnut tree down the road and I guessed he was remembering his own childhood in the village. The following day I had to go to Athens for a while and the next time I saw the café bar its door was locked and the windows dirty. One of its few regular customers was sitting disconsolately outside and he told me that Dimitri had decided to return to Athens with his wife and two daughters.

I didn't doubt that he would appear again some time in the future looking even more brusque and agitated. There was more money to be made in Athens, of course, and he had two daughters to marry, but he was Greek and wouldn't stay away for ever from his enchanted village where walnuts grew near a wild stream.

CHAPTER FOUR

$\mathcal{W}$E HAD EXPECTED TO FIND ANTONIS WORKING IN the house on our return from Athens but there was no sign of him although he had clearly been busy to marvellous effect. There had been no formal arrangement with him, and he had agreed to turn up only when he had time, but we were disappointed he wasn't there to show us more of his artistry. He had started in the little back room, which Marylle was planning to use as a study later, and had taken it into his head to decorate the stone ceiling in a way which obviously pleased him and, as it happened, us as well.

In fact, a part of the ceiling in this room was simply planks of wood above the round beams, but the rest of it consisted of great flat stones which had become dirty over the years. He had wire-brushed these clean before varnishing the beams and then, clearly under some kind of aesthetic compulsion, had used the rest of the varnish to paint a strange design on the stones. The effect was slightly hypnotic if you sat in a chair and looked up at the ceiling, as though the weird pattern was there to be deciphered before an extraordinary secret could be revealed.

As we grew to know Antonis better we realised that there was always going to be something surprising about him and that he could no more be relied on to do what was expected than the weather can be to stay the same. There was something infinitely changeable about him, which doesn't mean at all that he was unreliable, for he worked as hard in his own way as any of the vigorous old masons we employed. He was a force of nature in his own right but, unlike them, not stubborn and persevering, but lively, inventive and responsive to the materials with which he worked.

When we telephoned his wife to find out what had happened to him we were told that he had damaged his eye and couldn't work for a while. It turned out that he had stopped working on our house for a few days to repair the ceiling in one of the little churches around the valley and that a sharp piece of stone had fallen in his eye. He apologised for letting us down, she said, but expected to start work again shortly and, in the meantime, wanted to invite us to dinner at his house the following week.

It was the first time I had eaten at somebody's home on the island, other than at large formal occasions like wedding parties, and we turned up almost exactly on time, although Greeks do not usually regard punctuality as one of the cardinal virtues.

The house was high up above the valley and we drove to it along a tarmac road which had only been there for a couple of years. Of course there were steep paths down to the village, which were still used by those people without bicycles or cars, but the new road led through to other villages and was one of the island's minor traffic arteries now.

We had been instructed to park the car opposite a large fig tree and walk down some steps opposite it to where we would see a couple of white houses. When we turned the corner past a water deposit with a dead bird in it, Antonis's wife was waiting for us with a nervous smile on her face. We had met her once before in her working clothes but now she was wearing a floral dress and her broad face was rouged under ornate hair.

— I thought you might lose your way, she said. Antonis has gone to get some wine from one of our neighbours but he shouldn't be long.

She led the way down the path past one house and then up some steps to the terrace of another with a green and busy garden below it. We could see that a room inside the house was already laid for dinner but we sat on the terrace to admire the view while she brought drinks and assured us that Antonis would be along in a short while.

— He'd better be anyway, she added. The food will be ready in a few minutes.

When her husband still hadn't appeared twenty minutes later she was beginning to look flustered but carried her obvious embarrassment off with considerable aplomb.

— Of course Antonis is always liable to stop and talk to someone, she said loyally. It's not that he forgets what he's supposed to be doing but that he gets interested in other things.

Marylle reached for a dried fig and smiled at the woman.

— Don't worry about it, she said. We understand that Antonis is that kind of man. That's why we wanted him to work on the house.

The other woman looked at her anxiously.

— Are you happy with the work he's done so far then?

— We couldn't be more pleased. Have you seen it yourself?

— I was down there with him last week. To tell the truth, I wasn't sure he ought to have done the ceiling that way. It's not everyone that would like it but he always wants to do things differently.

When Antonis finally came up the steps from the path an hour after we had arrived he looked at us with surprise. He was carrying a litre bottle of draught wine under his arm but obviously didn't realise how long he had been, and blinked in surprise when his wife rushed into the kitchen to rescue the meal. It had dawned on him that he had kept us waiting when we all sat down at the table and he apologised as he poured out the wine by saying that he stayed to cut the hair of the man he had got it from.

It was the most novel excuse I had ever heard for someone turning up late but his wife seemed to accept it as perfectly reasonable.

— I forgot you had promised to do that for Leonidas, she said. How is he then?

Antonis nodded solemnly.

— He has to take it easy but he'll be all right in a few weeks.

When he saw me staring at him across the table he grinned slyly before picking up his glass of wine.

— I get this wine from a neighbour who had a hernia operation last week. It's very strong though and can knock you flat if you're not used to it.

— I'll bear that in mind, I said. I'm puzzled why he wanted you to cut his hair though.

The grin flickered out again as he dipped some bread into the sauce on his plate.

— I used to be a hairdresser, he explained. Nowadays I just cut people's hair around here in their homes.

There was a photograph of him on the sideboard against the wall and I could see that he hadn't changed much in appearance since it was taken. Of course he had his bad eye from the accident in the church now, which seemed to make him glare a little wildly, and his thin face was lined, but he was still the same dapper man in the picture. There was an elegance about him, from his immaculate silvery hair to his long artistic hands, even though he spent most of his days in tumbledown little churches in need of restoration. I don't know whether he was aware of me studying him but he looked up suddenly and pointed to the food on the table with his fork.

— Why are you not eating more? It is all from my garden and is the most pure and innocent food you will find.

It was true that everything on the table looked as though it had been alive and growing until only a few hours before. There was a salad of tomatoes and onions with fresh olive oil and oregano scattered over it, a dish of beans, stuffed courgette flowers again, and a chicken cooked with fresh vegetables that made the saliva run just to smell it. The bread was the only part of the meal that had been brought in from outside but, once soaked in juice from the other dishes, it tasted as though it had been baked for no other purpose than to ensure nothing of the meal was wasted. I drank the wine carefully and finished up with the happy feeling that I had just feasted at the green heart of creation.

There had been little talking during the meal, for food has to be honoured when it comes from your own garden, but afterwards Antonis said that he would start work in the house again in a couple of days' time.

He had brought along a number of tools when I saw him there next and I got the impression that he had decided to tackle several jobs for us whether we wanted him to or not. He had started on the beams in the front room but, when I had difficulty opening the door, stopped to repair the lock for me. The variety of tools, together with pots of varnish and paint, increased over the next few days until there was scarcely a shelf or old wooden chest that wasn't full of his tins and implements. When he had scoured the beautiful flat ceiling stones he stripped and varnished the beams, but then stopped to fix a couple of windows for us that wouldn't close properly before finishing the job in hand.

After a while I began to get the feeling that there wasn't anything broken, or in need of renovation, that he couldn't fix in one way or another. Watching him at work with his various

Antonis varnishing the pergola

appliances, I was reminded of that archetypal clown described by the Spanish essayist Ortega, who produced a new and different musical instrument from his great baggy pockets every time the ringmaster took one away from him. He was a symbol of mankind's ability to respond to adversity with spirit and creativity and, in a way, Antonis had the same kind of fertile wizardry as well.

Of course, he was also a musician like the exuberant clown, but I don't think he would have produced flutes and pipes with the same abandon in a similar predicament. Although he was infinitely resourceful, he didn't have the same optimism and prodigality. The clown makes a statement about the springy nature of humanity in general, but Antonis is a Greek and can feel very depressed and persecuted if he believes the fates are against him. There is a certain craftiness about him, and he can easily fall prey to dark suspicions, but he is, without a doubt, one of the most dexterous people I have ever met.

I cannot imagine a problem of a practical nature arising for which he couldn't produce an appropriate tool and the skill to use it. We had seen him as a violinist, weaving urgent island rhythms from his instrument, as a master craftsman working to restore ancient little churches, as a painter and locksmith, and it was easy to imagine him plying scissors and comb adroitly to shape the hair of his fellow villagers. I was walking near the house one day when I saw an old man grafting a fig tree and asked whether he knew someone I could hire to do the same job in our garden.

He straightened up with a theatrical groan and stared at me as though I was an idiot.

— The man working in your house now. Antonis is a master of many skills.

He was an expert gardener, of course, and had a knowledge of herbs and the edible wild greens of the countryside that only old women seem to have as a rule. I had walked past his sister's garden many times without spotting anything interesting, but one day he brought me a large bunch of sorrel he had picked there after she had gone back to Athens. Another time he produced a small stook of oregano and we scarcely had a meal for weeks after which wasn't decorated and flavoured with this most pungent of herbs.

I found it impossible to observe Antonis using his many practical talents without mourning my father and the millions like him who were victims of a rich industrial society with an insistence on the division of labour. Because of this my father had been trained as an electrician but he had almost none of the other skills necessary to survive if he wasn't protected by the illusion of permanent employment. Of course he was paid a living wage, as he used to call it, but to me all this meant was that he was paid to stop living as a human being. He had lost that ability to respond ingeniously to life which makes man the protean creature he is and had become simply a particular function within the system.

This fact gave a baffled and surly edge to his character in the end, whereas Antonis was capable of the kind of grace that comes from knowing how much life can give back. It was true that he could also be wary and mistrustful but, when he felt that the sun had come out again, had a kind of secret hilarity about him and a wild little smile would keep breaking out on his face. He knew that life has to be lived in the breach to experience its treasures and hadn't lost that sense of astonished gratitude which surely made us human beings in the first place.

He had finished all the beams now and was about to start on the stone floor tiles, which were stained and needed some kind of protection after being cleaned. We had been intrigued about what he would do with the ceiling in the front room, which had flat grey stones above the beams instead of the cop-per-flecked stones in the small room with the strange design. He had achieved a comparable effect, as it happened, but by using white plaster to create a similar pattern, had made the whole room seem more spacious and full of light.

It was agreed that he should use diesel oil on the floor tiles after sanding them down and we looked forward to seeing them after returning from another quick trip to Athens. A couple of hours before we were due to catch the ferry Antonis's wife rang up to say that he needed some of the money we owed him to buy new tools.

We said we could deliver it to them in the road up from their house but would have to drive straight on if they weren't waiting for us. When I pulled up under a fig tree an hour later they were both there and Antonis gave Marylle a basket of fat black figs they had just picked after accepting the money.

It was a simple present but expressed a perfect sense of that moment in the road and I could see that he knew it as he stepped back to incline his sleek head gravely.

— Have a safe journey. Kalo taxidi.

I shook his hand before we climbed back into the car.

— Can we bring you anything back from Athens?

He stared at me fiercely for a moment and then crossed himself in the fashion of the Orthodox Church.

— Just bring back yourself without harm.

When we had gone to London earlier in the year old Yorgo, the mason, had wished me the same thing and on the ferry later we had seen dolphins skipping along beside it. There were no dolphins to be seen this time but I was remembering Antonis' agile face as I stared into the torn silver sea.

The carpenter had been when we got back and a new low bed of knotted pine was waiting in the main bedroom for us. It was late September now and the weather was so warm and peaceful that Marylle and I decided to start living in the house even though there was still work going on. I stayed there most days keeping an eye on things while Marylle was talking to various people about an arts festival she was hoping to organise on the island.

I think it was Dora who had first thrown out the idea for a festival over dinner down by the sea the previous year. It hadn't really taken root, however, until a former London art school student with an interesting profile had arrived on holiday that summer. We had met Bambi Ballard in the village house of a painter from the island who now lived in Paris most of the year. It emerged gradually during the course of the evening that she had made clothes for the Rolling Stones, danced on a taverna table with all the players of a Greek football team, made a few passes in a bull ring, slept in a Turkish ditch, and generally led a more than ordinarily active life.

She was also living in Paris at that stage of her life and had become an expert on restoring great silent films. This had come about after she had first interested herself in the silent classic 'Napoleon' by Abel Gance. She had been in Athens to arrange a showing of the film with an orchestra playing a special score for it but had come to the island for a break by the sea.

When she heard about the festival from Marylle she was enthusiastic at once and started looking at possible locations for it the next day. Within a couple of weeks she had enthused a number of other people and put together a notional programme for the inaugural festival the following year. The main event was to be a performance of the great silent film 'The Wind' with Lilian Gish of the beautiful pleading eyes as its heroine. This takes place in a deserted part of the Wild West where life is achieved in the teeth of high gales and Bambi was proposing to show it with full orchestral accompaniment.

Other proposed events included a chamber concert, a couple of recitals in a ruined Byzantine chapel, and a production of a play by the Latin author Terence called the 'Woman of Andros'. The play is a witty farce about a young Athenian who has caused the full womb of a young lady wrongly supposed to be the sister of a courtesan from Andros. There appears to be no other reason for the play's title than this case of mistaken identity and the naughty island courtesan has died before the curtains open. It is tempting to think that Andros may have had a reputation for 'filles de joie' in classical times, and that the ladies who danced naked to encourage the silk worms were their lineal descendants, but probably the women were as respectable then as they are today.

Bambi had returned to Paris some weeks earlier but had left a vivid impression on those who had met her. They were used to English ladies of a certain age who arrived with small knapsacks and determined walking shoes but not, I think, someone with her style and energy. Although she walked about in the kind of minute denim shorts more conventionally sported by those closer to their youth, I always felt she had a lot in common with those intrepid Victorian ladies who wandered the globe with their umbrellas at the ready. She had the same kind of matter-of-fact independence, faith in her own mental and mechanical abilities, and a mild impatience with men who felt challenged by her brisk competence.

She was busy lobbying friends and European bureaucrats about the festival while Marylle was doing her bit on the island. I had promised vaguely to get involved somehow if it looked as though it would really happen, and one day Marylle took me to see a deserted water mill she thought might be converted into a recital hall.

The mill was at the end of a long beautiful path below a village where many sea captains live and was more spectacular than I had supposed. It was a ruin now, of course, and open to the sky, but its great wheel was still intact. The stream running just below the path didn't look as though it had ever flowed with enough force to turn it, though, because the huge gaunt monster must have been as high as a two-storey house. There were the remains of the mill's enormous dead engine inside the building and black timbers lying on the ground.

It was a marvellously romantic location but I hadn't the slightest idea of how the builders had managed to transport the materials up the little path, let alone the tremendous wheel itself. For the same reason I didn't see that it was going to be easy to turn the mill into a music palace without using an army of mules, and there weren't that many on the island any longer.

Antonis had finished the ceilings by now and promised that he would be available for more work when the plasterers had finished. He had to complete his restoration of the little church in the meantime and one day we dropped in to see him on the way to filling up our bottles with spring water. The last time we had looked inside the tiny chapel it had been full of dust and rubble but now a baby could have sat quietly on the floor without getting dirty.

It was late in the morning and his wife had just arrived with his packed lunch and, inevitably, they insisted that we shared it with them. There was no way they would let us refuse so we accepted a small cold fried fish each and stood there munching it in the minute but glowing church. The oil in the lamps shone almost fervently and the ornate wooden screen from behind which the priest would emerge when a service was held gleamed under its new coat of varnish.

I hadn't noticed until we got outside that Antonis was wearing a plastic bag to protect his hair as he worked but there seemed nothing odd about it at all. The next time we saw him he was sitting at a long table full of television cameramen and journalists on the terrace of a large hotel.

The reason we were there was for Marylle to meet a cameraman who had a house on the island and talk about the festival. It wasn't clear why Antonis was there but he nodded gravely to us as we sat down and just smiled enigmatically when he saw me looking down the table at him.

It was a week later when he turned up at the house and mentioned that he had been on television the previous evening.

— What were you doing?

— Playing the violin.

After a while it emerged that one of the Greek television stations was running a series of films on island customs and that he had played at a traditional Andros wedding feast.

I stared at him.

— Where did you learn to play the violin Antonis?

— My uncle taught me. He had a barber's shop not far from here and I learned to cut hair from him as well.

— Have you ever played it professionally?

— Only once. I was a cook on a merchant ship and decided to stay in America for six months after one voyage. I played at a big restaurant in Houston.

— How did you get on with the Americans?

— I didn't meet many. The restaurant was Macedonian and everybody who came was Greek.

I thought of him working away in the little chapel with his intent questioning face and nimble fingers.

— You've done a lot of different things in your life haven't you?

He shrugged.

— It's all work. That's what life's about isn't it?

The same pair of brown hawks were circling above the stream as we walked out on to the terrace and the shivering leaves on the big plane tree were beginning to turn rusty at the edges.

— I don't suppose you know anything about water mills?

He ground out his cigarette butt carefully before turning to smile at me.

— Why do you ask?

— There's an old mill down on the next level. We're very interested in getting it to work again some day if it's possible.

After inspecting the mute stony remains of the mill with me he glanced up at the slowly wheeling hawks before lighting another cigarette.

— I'll have a look at it when we've finished the rest of the work on the house. I think it can be fixed.

— How can you be sure?

— There was a mill in the house where I grew up. I remember how it worked.

The two partners who had rented the café bar at the top of the steps which Dimitri had run were having their inaugural opening that evening and Antonis left shortly afterwards to get ready. There had been some local excitement for several weeks because the new people had gone to quite a lot of trouble to smarten the place up. They had even built an elegant bar inside with exotic foreign bottles on the shelves and a pergola outside would eventually be draped by vines and climbing flowers.

The air was darkening as Marylle and I walked up to join the festivities and there was a warm sweetish smell in the valley from rotting figs. There had been figs drying on the flat roofs of the houses for most of the previous month and the village women would now be treating them with bay leaves and orange flower water to make offerings for visitors. The snack bar was crowded for the occasion and the food on offer was pizzas, which didn't interest us very much, but it was an opportunity for the villagers to get together. We had a drink with Antonis and his wife but then sat outside under the pergola to escape the noise from the bar's new record player.

CHAPTER FIVE

*T*HERE WAS SO MUCH SMOKE THAT I HAD COMPLETELY lost sight of Nico and could only vaguely make out his wife under one of the lemon trees waving her arms wildly as though to beat it away. There was no sign of flames either, although I knew that the fire had been burning fiercely only a few minutes earlier. I looked around to see other plumes of smoke across the valley and, when I turned back, saw Nico stumble out of the dark billowing clouds and wave to me with a wild toothless grin on his dangerous face.

It was well into October now and, although the rains hadn't come, there was still the lopped branches and other autumn detritus to burn before the winter. We hadn't asked Nico to do this but he had turned up a week before to hack away at the wild fig trees in a controlled fury. This morning he had piled dry material against the wall beneath the terrace and started the fire I had seen blazing earlier before throwing the green wood on it.

(There was nowhere else to burn it in our crowded little orchard, without danger of the fire getting out of control, but a couple of days later I found scarred and blind lemons on the trees nearest the flames).

There had been a moment or two as the fire licked around the fresh fig tree branches before biting into them and releasing the harsh choking brume of smoke. I had regarded Nico at a distance until then, if only because of his fierce countenance and physical strength, but now he seemed like some demented Greek spirit as he capered below me, born of the elements and full of manic glee.

As I stood there waving back at him and smiling at what I thought was his smoky excitement I realised he was trying to say something. It finally dawned on me that he wanted water as a precaution in case anything went wrong and I rushed to throw down the hose pipe to him and turn on the tap.

After grabbing it he plunged back into the thick inferno and emerged again a few minutes later to shout something at his wife. Then he bent his head to drink at the water pouring out of the green pipe and disappeared towards the house down by the bridge. We were friendly with the owners, who were a retired seaman and his wife, and knew that Nico did the occasional job for them as well.

When he didn't appear again for a while his wife batted her hands at the smoke and smiled cheerfully at me before beginning to pile up material for another fire against the wall on the path. It was clearly Nico's job to decide when it was safe to light the fires but, after he still hadn't returned ten minutes later, she took a box of matches from a huge pocket in her skirt and lit it herself. The smoke was starting to drift down towards the little bridge when Nico appeared and grunted something at her before looking at me.

— My wife is always in a hurry, he said. I was talking with the old couple.

— Will the fire be all right?

He glanced at it almost with distaste.

— Of course.

— Come in and have a coffee then.

— He's already had a coffee, said his wife. That's what he was doing down at the other house while we were waiting for him.

I would have been wary of talking to Nico like that but she had been married to him for a long time and his only reaction was to look a bit sheepish.

— I'll see you tomorrow then, he said to me. We have to feed the animals now.

Nico had been watering the orchard for us whenever it didn't rain for more than a year but we had only really got to know him in recent months. The watering involved digging trenches in the ground to make sure each fruit tree got the moisture it needed and diverting the flow of water from the communal channel to our garden. There was a system in the valley which ensured that each plot of land got water at least twice a week from the channel but someone had to be there to open up the side trenches. Nico had been recommended to us after the first man we had hired to look after the orchard had fallen ill.

It was only later that we discovered he could be useful to us in many other ways as well. I doubt whether anyone knew what was happening in the valley as well as Nico since he spent most of his time in it one way and another. He was more or less self-sufficient, like several of the villagers, but, as well as his other animals, he owned the mules which were the only real form of transportation in the valley.

Appearances can be deceptive, of course, but in Nico's case they were positively treacherous. The first couple of times I met him I was convinced that he was probably cruel and violent, simply because he had that kind of face and a rough careless voice. Only after a while did it dawn on me that his mules were obviously well-looked after and that his two sons, who sometimes came to water the trees in his place, were hardworking lads and apparently free from the usual teenage problems and resentments.

He was also immensely strong and this gave me the wrong

impression about him as well, for I couldn't look at him without being convinced that he was enormous. It was only when I began to like him that I realised he was almost slim and not very big at all. In fact, when he sat on the stool in our kitchen, doubled up with laughter at something one of the masons had said, he looked on the small side and mischievous rather than threatening.

The problem was his face which, at first sight, seemed like one of those masks designed to suggest that the beast still has a part to play in human nature. Since Nico usually wore a black peaked cap, this wild and menacing aspect could seem even more grimly etched into his features and I have seen much bigger men walk the other way once they had observed that he didn't seem best pleased with life.

This savage appearance was only a simple caricature though and, when his face was animated, it tended to collapse into a series of quite comical separate features. He had fairly large ears for a start and a moustache that drooped at each side of his mouth. The grey and black curls that escaped on either side of his cap suggested wild and luxuriant hair, but when he removed the cap, it was as coarse and patchy as couch grass.

It was the nose that contributed most to the impression of cruelty, since it was hawked and jutting to a degree. By the same token it took up much more room on his face than the average nose and, when looked at in isolation, seemed clumsy and forlorn. The trouble was that it dominated the landscape of his face to such an extent that, like an escarpment in a fertile plain, it apparently indicated danger rather than reassurance.

There was no doubt that he could look highly forbidding, however, and especially when he was astride one of his mules. He was by nature a worrying man and what was really a thoughtful expression on his face could look like a high commanding frown when he was in the saddle.

It was probably fortunate for the more nervous people who met him that he had only a few teeth left, all of which seemed

5 ROBERT LEIGH, *Sunlight in the wine*

to be crowded to one side of his mouth. This meant that when he laughed, which, it is true, wasn't very often, he could suddenly change from a man of apparent severity to one prone to helpless giggles.

(I have never worked out why gap-toothed mouths can make some men look vulnerable and funny while in others dramatically underscore their obvious brutality. It is difficult to imagine Bill Sykes or Fagin, for instance, with a full mouth of healthy teeth, and I'm quite certain that Stalin must have had nasty dental problems.)

The first time I had really got to know Nico was when he and his brother the priest had been co-opted by Yorgo to help in the construction of our new roof. It had been obvious then that he was exceptionally strong for a man of nearly fifty but we didn't realise how much until our new kitchen was installed. Since everything had to come down the steep path to our house I was anticipating all kinds of difficulties. We had hired Nico to help but his mules could only carry materials which could be fitted into their deep panniers or strapped equitably on either side of their horned saddles. It had not occurred to me that Nico himself shared some of his mules' basic qualities, including sure-footedness and balance as well as strength. In addition, of course, he had a fund of ingenuity and resourcefulness, together with the ability to remember and draw conclusions.

(I have a feeling that the most important aspect of the Greek experience in Western culture lies in its conviction that solutions can be found to the problems with which living presents us. We are fascinated by the myths, most of which, I suspect, reflect their more fatalistic Asiatic origins, but what endures is the dawning human optimism and the slow stubborn growth of reliable techniques.)

It may sound a bit ridiculous to sound this note when talking about Nico but, in his own way, he was a man of faith and a technician of a kind. I hadn't realised, when we had asked

Nico on one of his mules

him to bring down the kitchen parts, that he would make sensible arrangements based on similar tasks he had handled in the past. He had conscripted another one of his brothers to help, as well as his two sons, and supervised everything himself with a confidence that made all seem possible. When it came to the more difficult kitchen furniture, such as the refrigerator and stove, he carried them himself. This involved strapping them on his back with rope, which he could pull down for added tension with each hand, before walking down the steps bent almost double.

(There is no lack of competitive pride among Greek men and, when Antonis, who was working in the house at the time, saw this, he rushed out and appeared ten minutes later carrying a kitchen cabinet on his own slimmer back.)

This was all very impressive to someone like me, who hasn't had to rely on physical strength to survive in life, but child's play compared to what happened when the marble working surfaces were delivered. There were five of these, in various shapes, of which the largest was two metres long and weighed more than one hundred and sixty kilos. Nico organised this by improvising a wooden stretcher from four pieces of wood and tying the huge slab of marble to it with rope. With a man at each corner of the stretcher it was then relatively simple to manhandle it down the steps, although more of a problem to get it through the door into the kitchen.

The smaller surfaces presented less of a problem but I wasn't sure how he would handle the second largest piece, which was eighty kilos in weight. When I went up the steps to check what solution he had devised for carrying this I almost bumped into him coming the other way. He was stooped and bow-legged again with the great plank of shiny stone on his back. There were no ropes this time but he was gripping it with both hands behind him while his older son walked beside him to stabilise it.

When he had got it into the kitchen Nico turned to me with

a huge grin and his face pouring with sweat. He knew I was impressed and was obviously feeling pleased with himself.

— That's the way I make my living, he said as he wiped his face with the sleeve of his shirt. I do whatever makes me sweat a lot. Now I'll have a coffee if you've got any.

There was scarcely a day in the valley when I didn't see Nico going around the paths with one or all three of his mules. He would be taking sacks of lemons from one of the larger orchards to be delivered somewhere, logs of wood to be stacked for winter fireplaces, bags of cement up to where a new house was being built, and anything else that had to be carried through the steep and narrow valley paths.

At the same time he had his own work to do for, like many other villagers, he was up before dawn every morning to tend his animals before going out to do his other job. After I became friendly with him I learned that he had a whole range of useful farmyard animals, including sheep as well as goats and chickens, and enough land to justify six water deposits. After he decided he was friendly with us, and not just an occasional hired hand, he would leave bags of marrows and other vegetables tied to the front door handle, and we became regular buyers of his delicious soft cakes of white goats' cheese.

His two sons were bulkier versions of himself, although less direct and focused physically, and were both apprenticed at building trades that would provide them with a better start in life than Nico himself had.

He told me one evening over a glass of beer that he had worked as a sailor on merchant ships after leaving school, like many men of his generation on the island. They were lucky in a way that the island had bred so many shipowners because there was almost no other form of employment in those days and even cigarettes were cheap when you were at sea.

This meant that he could save up to get married, which he did after being a sailor for fifteen years, and then work as hard as possible to buy more land and animals.

There was something quite different about Nico from the other men we had got to know well like Yorgo and Antonis. It was not simply that they were masters of crafts and that his virtues were those of the labourer who had become a man of property through sheer hard work. He was respectful towards them, of course, and listened attentively to what they said, but I always had the feeling that his attitude towards life was more combative, even though I never saw him raise a hand to man or animal.

The relationship he had with his own animals seemed demanding but almost courteous to me, like an employer who expects people to work extremely hard for him but treats them with respect and even affection as well. He wasn't the slightest bit sentimental towards them but I thought sometimes that he valued them as creatures more than most human beings. They had those qualities of sheer physical strength and athleticism that he clearly admired most in life.

I never got to know the name of his third mule but the other two were called Kokkino, which is Greek for red, and Psaroula, meaning grey-haired, although the animal in question was over fourteen hands high, and handsome into the bargain. All three could move like greased lightning when they weren't carrying heavy loads, and the sight of Nico careering down the street on one of them, his moustache quivering delightedly on his lip, wasn't easy to forget.

It was only when I remembered reading somewhere that ancient Hellenic physical types are found more often in the Cyclades than elsewhere that I became convinced that Nico really was descended from this race. I'm sure he'd be embarrassed to hear me say it but it always seemed to me that he had honour as well as courage in his person. It was difficult to imagine him letting anyone down he respected. Marylle certainly thought he had 'levendia', which is usually translated as manliness but has a bit of whatever Sir Lancelot had thrown in as well.

He was always willing to take on any work to augment family finances and I have a vivid memory of him as a waiter at the café bar during a village festival when Dimitri was still renting it. There were tables out in the street and Dimitri was running around with sweat apparently pouring from his eyes. The only two other people serving were his daughters but Nico moved around with the calm certainty of a boxer soliciting donations at a church service.

He wasn't the slightest bit flustered by the numbers of people demanding attention and I was glad of his presence a little while after we had sat down. A large car tried to edge through, even though the street was crowded, and clipped me on the elbow as I sat at our table.

I have managed to learn some Greek but the driver obviously didn't approve of the term I used when I shouted at him. He stopped the car at once and was marching back when Nico looked up and came over towards us with a preparatory waggle of his shoulders.

The man took one look at him and stared at me in horror for a moment before climbing hastily back into his car.

The weather was still marvellous although there was gloom among the villagers about what the lack of rain would do to the olives. We were enjoying it, of course, and Marylle swam almost every day in water that rose around her like calm green silk, but it was true that summers don't usually last that long even in Greece.

The freak conditions were causing strange convulsions in the valley and I walked out of the house one day to find it drowning in butterflies. I have never seen so many in my life and, when I stopped at one shimmering bush, there were several on each of its many thousand leaves. They moved away in a dense vibrant cloud of giddy wings and settled gracefully back to their extraordinary feasting the moment I moved on up the path.

Later that morning I sat on the terrace with my cup of coffee watching the entire valley heave beneath them. There were so many that the air seemed to be full of coloured rain yet I didn't recall seeing more than one or two the day before.

The lizards were obviously enjoying this dramatic Indian summer as well and there were thousands sunning themselves on the tops of the stone walls in the valley paths.

It had been many years since I had been long enough in the countryside to become fascinated by its dramas again and the next few days I spent as an absorbed spectator. There was a small tragedy one morning when a dove suddenly fell out of the sky into our orchard. I watched with useless pity as it looked around it dazedly and struggled to lift itself again into the murmuring air. Finally, I had to stun it by knocking its head against the steps and then twist its feathered neck.

Another afternoon I was chipping away at the cement between the stones in the terrace wall when I looked up to see a fully-grown stork sailing down towards the fields on the other side of the stream. I had time only to remark that it seemed to be craning its long neck to see where it should land before it disappeared behind a plane tree.

When I described it to one of the plasterers later he confirmed that it was a stork and was probably flying up to winter on one of the Thracian lakes in Northern Greece.

The same plasterer also told me that the valley was full of small animals whose name I didn't recognise but turned out to be martens. I don't remember ever seeing one of these bushy-tailed creatures before, even in Somerset, but soon learned to recognise their nervous nocturnal screams and spotted droppings on the terrace every morning.

Of course the birds were as confused as the islanders themselves and were still chattering excitedly as I sat on the terrace with my ouzo in the early darkness. There were a few who were strange to me but most were familiar and included robins, sparrows, wagtails, blackbirds, crows and the occasional whirring puzzled partridge. The nightingales were in the trees higher up the valley but their rapturous song echoed around it most nights like a call to something I had forgotten might still be there.

The first days of November came but the sky remained blue and cloudless. The leaves on some of our fruit trees were beginning to turn down in despair and Marylle spent hours spraying them from the terrace with the hose pipe. Because of the strange weather a plague of insects attacked the oranges and we were told that a tiny worm would start infesting them within a few weeks. The only thing to do was to use those that had already been punctured by the insects for orange juice as soon as possible.

Further down the valley the trees seemed to smoulder like a quiet green fire in the late afternoons with shoots of autumn colours in its depths. The yellow leaves of a pomegranate tree glowed in the distance and, nearer to the house, the red leaves of what Antonis said was a jujube tree. I believed him, of course, but still have no clear idea what a jujube is, even after the dictionary revealed that it was an edible berry-like drupe, whatever that may be.

It was easy to become lulled by the peaceful sun but winter wasn't far away and the house would need heating before long. Nico had delivered us a small mountain of olive tree branches a week before and we were waiting for him to saw them into logs for the three fireplaces in the house. He turned up one morning with Yanni, his eldest son, his younger brother the priest, and a power saw, which he raised in both hands to salute me, like some friendly warrior proud of his newfangled weapon.

It turned out that the saw belonged to his brother, or, at least, that he was the one most competent to use it, for it was he who wielded it for the next few hours, with Yanni gingerly holding the branches down for him. It was only the second time I had seen the tough little priest without his clerical dress and his bearded face was fierce with concentration as the logs slowly piled up.

I had to fetch him cold water to drink a number of times during the morning and it was only when we were talking in the house later that he told me he had diabetes. It didn't seem to bother him and he happily drank some brandy even though I told him that I didn't think it was wise.

A couple of days later Nico was helping me clear some vegetation from the top of the stone wall on the other side of the path outside the house. At one point he dug out a twisted root of some kind and laid it almost reverentially on the ground.

I looked at the black woody thing with suspicion.

— What plant is that from?

— I don't know but I remember my grandmother tying one on a wooden cross to protect against the evil eye.

(The 'evil eye' delivers a curse born from envy and is believed in to such an extent in Greece that the Orthodox Church recognises it and even practises a ceremony to exorcise it).

This made me think of Papa Philippos but, when I asked after him, Nico said that he had been taken to Athens by helicopter the day before and was in a special hospital reserved for sick priests.

— What on earth happened to him?

— He was taken ill and they found a lot of sugar in his blood at the clinic. The trouble is he wasn't taking any notice of what the doctors told him.

— How is he now?

He's all right but they're having to give him insulin through a tube.

— He'd better do what the doctors say in future. A diabetic can easily have kidney failure or go blind.

I had thought of diabetics as prone to weight loss and physical weakness until then but that certainly wasn't true of Nico's brother. He could seem almost sedate in his black robe

– 74 –

and hat but, when sawing our logs in jeans and plaid shirt with a crucifix swinging around his corded neck, had looked like someone you wouldn't think had been ill in his life.

Although it was still hot the sky had been cloudy for the last couple of days and, suddenly, like bullets in heaven, a few drops of hard rain began to hit the earth on the stone wall. Nico looked up with astonishment and pleasure as it began to rain quite hard and we scuttled indoors for coffee and brandy.

After more than six months of almost flawless sunshine it was strange to look out of the door and see the path exploding with raindrops and Nico seemed almost dazed by the sight. He rushed out when there was a lull and it was several days before I saw him again, although I glimpsed him on one of his mules across the valley occasionally when the clouds parted for a while.

It rained until the end of the week and a lot of this time I could have been found on the terrace under an umbrella staring down at the stream. It had been sprightly enough even in the hot months of the summer but now it was spitting and kicking wildly as it bolted down past the house. I wasn't at all surprised when Antonis turned up one afternoon and said that it used to overflow its banks quite often when he was a boy.

When I spoke to Nico the following week he said that his brother was out of hospital now and was staying at his house so that his wife could look after him. A couple of days later I was coming down the path from the village when I saw Philippos himself standing in his garden looking out over the quiet valley.

He looked as sturdy as ever and it was easy to forget that he was a priest but when I said that he would have to take better care of himself in the future he just shrugged.

— We must not forget that it is God who decides when we leave this earth, he said. I have my duties to perform and cannot spend all my time worrying about what might happen if I get ill again.

CHAPTER SIX

$\mathcal{T}$HE FIRST TIME I VISITED ANDROS WITH MARYLLE several years ago we drove up to a mountain village where we dropped in for a drink at a little café bar. It was shortly before Easter and among the men standing at the bar was a sturdy old man carrying a rifle and hunting bag. He had one of those marvellous Greek faces that seem set in wrinkled stone and looked as though he had spent all his life on the island. When we got talking to him, however, it turned out that he had also been a sailor for some years and spoke English of a kind.

When he learned that I was living in London at the time he remarked that he had been there twice and the second time had found his way to Piccadilly. He added that it was fortunate that there had been so many priests around because one of them had showed him how to get back to the dock where his ship was waiting.

I had never seen more than the occasional priest in the West End at any one time and looked at Marylle in puzzlement before turning back to him.

— Are you sure he was a priest?

— Well, he had a priest's hat on and was dressed in black, even though he didn't wear a robe.

It was only then that I realised the old man had been helped on his way by a policeman, whose black conical helmet must have looked to him like the tall black hat worn by priests of the Orthodox Church. I didn't tell him he had been mistaken, of course, not only because it would have been patronising but also because I liked the idea that he believed London was full of friendly priests.

Nor did I find it surprising that he thought this because there are many priests in Greece and he probably assumed it was normal everywhere. More to the point, they are priests who are very visible members of the community, instantly recognisable with their black robes and beards, even if some, like Papa Philippos, do look a bit fiery for men of the cloth.

There were so many priests in Greece when it achieved liberation from the Turks in the last century that attempts were made to reduce numbers although it can't have been easy. The vast majority were parish priests from small villages all over the country and many of them, particularly in the Peloponnese, had been active in fighting against their Turkish occupiers. Although it is supposed to be harder to qualify for office today, it isn't obvious that there are fewer priests around, and there are three to be found quite often in our little village alone.

They don't all practise in the village itself of course but either live in it or, at least, near enough to it to be considered residents of the area. The last time I ran into all three together was when the festival of the village church was held in Dimitri's café bar. It struck me then that it would be difficult to imagine three more different characters in priests' robes, although each, so far as I could see, was equally committed to his vocation and the welfare of the people he served.

The most important of the three, on that occasion, was Papa Andreas, who was the priest of the village itself and had been conducting services at its church that day. He was also the eldest of them, with a salt and pepper beard, and a gentle smile which charmed me, even though he was also the most inquisitive. I gathered that the other two had become priests out of personal need, but Papa Andreas had also followed the family tradition in that both his father and grandfather had been parish priests before him.

I had already become quite friendly with him because his own house was not far from our cottage and I was used to bumping into him on the valley paths. He had his own land and animals, like most of the other villagers, and spent much of his time working in his fields, although I never saw him without his 'soft' priest's hat, which is a sort of informal version of the one usually worn.

It was clear that he was popular among the villagers and it was easy to see why. A burly man in his late fifties, who once told me he did physical jerks every morning to keep fit, there was also something comfortable and reassuring about him. He wore a patterned woollen pullover every time I saw him in the valley and, when I asked him once what he was carrying in a large paper bag, he told me with a smile that it was a treat made from the seeds of the cotton plant for his sheep who were grazing in a nearby field.

At the festival he was sitting with an erect thinner priest called Papa Leonidas who lived at the top of the valley but who officiated at a village church several kilometres away across the mountain. I had only spoken to him a couple of times before but had been struck by how clever and articulate he was compared to other parish priests I had met. There was a slightly world-weary air about him, however, and I wasn't completely surprised to find out later that he had been a captain on a merchant ship not long before.

I have no idea why he left the sea to become a priest in a small village but he must have taken a substantial fall of income in the process. Although priests are paid from central

Pappa Philippos and Papa Andreas

funds nowadays, instead of receiving tributes from their parish-
ioners as in the past, it is barely enough to live on and run a
second-hand car as a rule. I had the notion that he was a man
exhausted by the burden of command, and perhaps by some
personal tragedies of his own, but I had no means of knowing.
It was just that he looked a little chastened, even ascetic,
although he smoked too much to suggest he had left all his
secular cares behind him.

It is difficult to give a clear picture of Papa Leonidas
because, like many men who have spent time in the larger
world, he had flattened himself out to some extent and was no
longer easy to read. This was most emphatically not true of
Papa Philippos, however, who was certainly not given to
introspection and couldn't help making an impression on people around him. He was sitting at a different table to his two
fellow priests at the café bar and, when we walked in, was
slapping his knee fiercely as he roared in helpless laughter
about something another man had told him.

He was the last person I would have suspected of being a
priest had I not known him, not only because of his rough
appearance, but because of his clear enjoyment of all that is
rude and elemental in life. It took me some time to realise that
this was essentially nothing more than a hearty form of reverence and that village people would be able to relate easily to a
priest with his demonstrable talent for satisfaction. This is what
made it a little sad when his illness forced him to become more
spartan in his habits, although it didn't stop him taking
pleasure in other people's appetites. A couple of weeks after he
had left hospital I ran into him at the café bar, where he had
been using the telephone, and he insisted on buying me two
ouzos and piling up my plate with mezedes while he himself
had just a soft drink.

I never saw him together with his wife but the majority of
parish priests in Greece are married with children of their own.
It seems to me that they are expected to fit comfortably into

their communities and it is probable that most country women would feel embarrassed with a priest who didn't have experience of married life and the spoils of the flesh. It is true that a priest isn't allowed to marry once he has been ordained, but the Greek genius for evading the strict letter of the law means that a man isn't stopped from becoming a clergyman if he is married already.

There are no doubt reasons for this which have as much to do with Greek historical experience as matters of dogma and ecclesiastical law. It is clear that the country owes a huge debt to the parish priests who helped keep their communities together under the Turkish occupation. Although many of them were almost illiterate, they were usually the only people to give children the rudiments of secular and religious education, often under difficult or even dangerous conditions. I always think of Papa Philippos as being exactly that kind of rough but determined priest and it is as difficult to imagine him being celibate as beer without froth on its top.

The fact that Greek priests can be married is one of the ways in which they differ from Roman Catholic priests, of course, but I have the feeling that where they really diverge is in the view they take of their own power. I was brought up in the Church of England but always admired the way Roman Catholic priests were prepared to accept and forgive even the extremes of human behaviour. It was only after a while that it occurred to me how much authority this gave them and, even more to the point, that it derived primarily from their rigorous abstinence from sex. The assumption seemed to be that, since human nature is thought to be indelibly corrupted by sex, the priest who embraces celibacy has earned the right to chastise or forgive the clumsy sinners in his flock.

The Greek priest lays claim to no such power on the other hand and appears to regard his role more as one of pleading on behalf of his fellow human beings than standing in judgement on them. He takes confession like a Roman Catholic priest, for instance, but has no real authority to absolve a penitent himself, and, unless he is feeling very arrogant, should properly confine himself to praying to God that the poor sinner might be forgiven.

There appears to be far less interest generally within the Greek Church in 'human depravity', in fact, and, so far as I can make out, it is not even necessary to believe that the Virgin Mary herself was entirely free from original sin. The emphasis appears to be much more on the notion of holiness, which has less to do with sexual renunciation than an inward quality of devotion and goodness, although it is true it is usually thought that monastic clergymen, who are unmarried, are more holy than others.

These priests are technically attached to monasteries, as their title suggests, but in practice, many have been ordained to conduct church services in the normal way, and it is from their ranks that bishops are ordinarily appointed. The first I met was when Marylle's seventy eight year old mother, who died at her home outside Athens, was brought to Andros to be buried in the family vault. It might have been a very sad occasion, of course, but she had lived a full life and would undoubtedly have suffered more if she hadn't died in her sleep. There were three clergymen at the cemetery chapel but the one I got to know best was an austere and saintly priest called Papa Yanni, who was a friend of the family.

It may have been because of the solemnity of that occasion that afterwards I always found Papa Yanni a little formidable, although he was usually polite and friendly to me. There was something remote about him, even when he was at social occasions or with children, and I imagine this was because he could never forget that he was a priest. It would be unfair to say that the average parish priest was not so wedded to his calling, but it was obviously a compelling vocation to Papa Yanni and it was clear that he was very conscious of his responsibilities to the people around him.

Although the beautiful church at which he officiated was at a village a little way out of Chora, he seemed to turn up everywhere in that corner of the island, and was clearly respected by both rich and poor. A slim dapper man, with attentive eyes and a neat greying little beard, I used to see him quite often walking up and down the main street in Chora like some anxious spiritual policeman. I don't know how many times he patrolled the town, but he must have covered a lot of miles every day, and every time he saw me he would wave with a short chopping motion across his chest as though giving a benediction of a kind.

I would occasionally see him striding out in the road leading out of the town as well and realised after a while that he didn't have a car and walked everywhere. He may have looked immaculate, with his crisp black robe and polished shoes, but he clearly didn't spend much money on his own needs and Antonis, who doesn't waste kind words about people, once told me he gave most of it to the poor.

He did have a smart black umbrella of his own though, because I saw him with it up one day when I drove past a tree where he was sheltering from a brief shower. He was standing as erect as a sentry and staring out blindly over the fields as he clearly contemplated some image deep inside himself. I opened the car window to ask him if he wanted me to take him somewhere but he looked at me so strangely that I closed it again and drove on.

I always got the impression with Papa Yanni that he regarded his primary duty as ministering to people rather than defending the strict articles of his faith. There was a look of compassion about him rather than schoolmasterly fanaticism but I don't doubt he could have lectured me at length about tradition and doctrine had my Greek been good enough. It is difficult for someone from another country to appreciate how much the history of Greece is bound up with its religion and I only realised this myself after reading a book on the subject I picked up one day.

There was a Christian community in Greece after its conversion by St Paul long before Constantinople was made the capital of a Roman Empire now officially embracing the Christian faith. Although the western half of the empire began to collapse under barbarian invasions soon after this the Pope in Rome was still regarded as the spiritual leader of Christendom. When a theological row broke out between Rome and Constantinople in the ninth century, however, the Greeks, who, after all, possessed the gospels written in their own language, allied themselves with the Patriarch in Constantinople.

The real break between the Church of Rome and the Greek Orthodox Church happened in the eleventh century when Constantinople was the brilliant capital city of the Eastern empire, and its language and culture was Greek. Several disputes about dogma were involved, but the main reason appears to have been a matter of pride again, with the Pope insisting that everybody else defer to him and the Patriarch accusing the Church of Rome in turn of heresy. Any hope of reunion vanished a century later when Constantinople was sacked by the crusaders and Greeks who refused to accept Papal authority were forced into exile. The new Roman Catholic bishop of Athens even had to be scolded by the Pope of the time for persecuting Orthodox Greeks too vigorously.

I don't suppose Papa Philippos was familiar with this history in detail but he would have certainly known about the main disagreement with the Roman Catholic Church, which hasn't changed in centuries. This is still to do with the status of the Pope, who the Greeks have always been willing to regard as the first bishop in Christendom because of the pre-eminence of Rome, but not at all as the absolute and final judge of all matters doctrinal and spiritual.

Papa Philippos might even have been able to explain to me the true significance of another dogmatic difference between the Churches, which is an assertion about the true provenance of the Holy Ghost and led to the Pope being told he was a heretic in the first place. The only other area of dispute I could discover myself concerned the Greek practice of using leavened bread at Eucharist whereas the Roman Catholics insist on unleavened.

(I was given a loaf of this bread which had been left over one Sunday morning and was intrigued by the device with three panels stamped on its crust. When I asked Papa Leonidas about it he explained that the central panel was for Jesus Christ, the right hand one the various saints, and the left hand panel the Virgin Mary.)

I would have felt bored reading about these minor doctrinal squabbles if I had not realised by then how treacherous and uncertain life has always been for the Greek people. It would have been even worse a couple of thousand years ago, and the promise of eternal bliss if they followed the right path of Christian orthodoxy must have meant that these tiny points of dogma were incredibly important. There has always been this attachment to the notion of proper initiation and spiritual training among Greeks anyway, since the ancient mystery cults.

It may be because of the same insecurity that the Greeks also feel that there are always ghosts of a kind to be appeased if tragedies are not to strike too often in this life. It's easy to think that this is just superstition at first, but the fact is that many developments in western thought passed Greece by while it was under Turkish occupation for more than four hundred years. The result is that Greeks haven't really lost their sense that human reason cannot explain everything and I, for one, feel comfortable with this attitude, even if it can lead to weird consequences sometimes.

There is no doubt that country priests like Papa Philippos genuinely understand how people still feel haunted and respond to it to a large extent. Not long ago Marylle and I stopped by the side of the road in another part of the island to watch a parish priest blessing a car which someone had obviously just bought.

When we met the same priest later I asked him whether it was normal to bless a consumer product but he just looked at me in surprise.

— The owner is a friend of mine and wanted protection for his car, he said. He saved up for years to buy it and is afraid people might be jealous of him.

I had forgotten about the 'evil eye', and the extent to which Greek people of all classes behave as though there are spirits around every corner which need to be placated with the right words. There are talismanic phrases in the language for almost every one of life's fateful moments, including my own favourite, which can be roughly translated as 'good getting up in the morning'.

This side of the Greek character probably also explains in part the vast numbers of icons in churches and private houses, not to mention those on sale in galleries and souvenir shops, for, as far as I can determine, excessive reverence of them is theoretically forbidden by the Church authorities. They are everywhere in Greece, however, and the mediaeval belief in the miraculous power of these glowing images still persists today among rich and poor alike. The Greek people have dark and ancient roots, and it is quite possible that these strange but hypnotic portraits of saints and martyrs have become fused in their souls with the local pagan deities they used to worship at one time.

The spiritual attraction of icons is strongest among country people, or those least influenced by the apparently rational content of language, and even the most remote and poor little church always has at least one.

I remember going for a walk with Marylle once along a part of the Andros coast and coming across a tiny little church at the end of a rough peninsula of rock. It was miles from anywhere but, when we pushed open the door, there was an old lady inside with her lips pressed against a cheap representation of one of the saints, which had been framed and hung on the white peeling wall.

Of course pagan rituals have been loosely buried under religious customs ever since Pope Julius I decided in the fourth century that Jesus was born on December 25th because it was already the date of a popular festival. It seems strange when the custom is presided over by a priest as cool and elegant as Papa Yanni, however, as I realised when he agreed to conduct mass in the little cemetery chapel on the anniversary of Marylle's mother's funeral.

After it was over we went outside and were handed little paper bags of food which are normally provided at these services for the dead, although I noticed that Papa Yanni didn't take one of them himself. The little snack was sweet on the tongue and I discovered later that it is traditionally made from boiled wheat, sugar and pomegranate seeds.

I am not a scholar but I would wager the whole of our next year's crop of lemons that these ingredients have been eaten when people are buried since the beginning of pagan times.

There is nobody more correct and generous in other matters than Papa Yanni, however, and he simply shook his head when Marylle offered to pay church expenses for the service and walked away with one of those courtly little waves of his white hand.

The impulse to placate the fates, in whatever form they show themselves, probably lies to some extent behind the extraordinary number of little churches, some no larger than a garden shed, which are scattered all over Greece. I doubt whether anyone knows exactly how many there are and a lot of them are built in places that are virtually inaccessible, or at least, not easy to reach, while others are perched beautifully in spots of great natural beauty. There is one high on top of a cliff in Andros with a view over the sea and down to the town of Chora with its harbour. It was built on that site together with the tomb of a member of one of the great shipping families of the island.

These tiny churches, which are usually locked to protect against thieves and vandals, but are in theory open for any worshipper to use, were mostly built by individuals or their families. Each one is an act of homage, a prayer in stone, and, since many were built while the country was occupied by the Ottoman Turks, there was probably reason enough for them. When I close my eyes and imagine these brilliant little cubes of white stone everywhere in Greece I always think of them as like the dragon's teeth in the myth, each urgent with the desire for more Christian churches to spring from the same Greek soil.

I suppose that under the Turkish occupation the Greek people began to identify even more strongly with the Orthodox Church and that every act of discrimination by Muslim against Christian helped shape their growing sense of national awareness. I don't know of a single Greek today who doesn't feel loyal to the Church as a national institution, whether he attends services regularly or not, or even is an atheist.

The priests continue to have an essential role in the community in administering those great rituals which have served to bind people together over the centuries. The most important of these for people who are not regular churchgoers are, in reverse order, the funeral service, the rites of holy matrimony, and baptism. They are each conducted with great solemnity and, at least to people not used to such ceremonies, seem to go on for ever.

I have been to a couple of weddings since coming to Greece and each time was amazed at the endurance showed by both bride and groom. The service is interminable and for part of the time as they stand there listening to the priest, they both wear garlands around their heads which are linked by a white ribbon to symbolise their new state of togetherness. At the climax of the ceremony they are supposed to dance three times around a table, on which is the Bible and communion wine, proceeded by the priest and followed by the maid of honour and best man.

When you consider the fact that there is always a huge gathering of relatives and friends afterwards, at which the nervous couple have to dance alone in front of everyone, it's a wonder that most people get married as early as they do.

There is no doubt that the most emotional ritual for Greeks is baptism, however, not only because the child is always the centre of attention in this country, but because the ceremony of giving it a name brings almost everything they care deeply about together into one hectic squalling act of living theatre.

For a start, the baby is a new member of the Greek community and, in a country that has lived under the yoke for centuries, this is enough reason for a celebration. The community in Greece lives through the names of its people, moreover, and renews itself at every baptism, because the child usually takes the same name as one of the grandparents or a very close relative. Since this custom has been the same far back into the country's past, it has managed to achieve a miraculous continuity through even the worst periods of its rough and tumultuous history.

The last baptism Marylle and I were invited to in Andros was for the six months old child of a sea captain and his wife who live in our village. The service in the church which stands opposite the walnut trees and above the marble steps was conducted by Papa Andreas and, since he is a friend of the family, Papa Yanni was also there to help as well. There were a lot of people both in the church and outside but we managed to be inside for the moving and dramatic heart of the sacrament.

It was the third baptism I had been to in Greece and it seems clear to me at least that the service has as much to do with the need for ritual within the community as the presentation of the child to God, since it is also extremely long, much to the baby's evident and audible discomfort. This is further compounded by the fact that the mother is not allowed to take part in the ceremony, and the baby spends most of its time in the arms of other people it clearly doesn't trust nearly as much.

The child we saw baptised in our village church was rather jolly and patient as it happened, and seemed much more interested in why so many people were making idiotic faces at him and, occasionally, stepping forward to touch him, than in what Papa Andreas was droning on about. It was only when the ceremony approached its climax, and he was undressed before being handed to the strange man in the black robes and funny hat that, not unreasonably, he began to suspect the worst and cry with heartbreaking abandon.

I gather that a priest would have held him by the nose and immersed him completely in water in times past, but the power of maternal indignation has been felt in the land in recent years, and now the usual custom is just to sit the child in the font for a couple of moments.

This is what happened in our village church at any event before the godfather stepped forward to anoint the baby liberally with oil, making a mess of himself as well in the process. I remember reading once that the oil for baptisms is flavoured by forty herbs and has to be blessed by the Patriarch at Constantinople before being sent out for sacramental use. I have no idea of whether that is still true today and don't imagine that the godfather cared very much about where it came from at that moment either.

After this the baby was wrapped in a large warm towel and handed to his mother to be dressed in fresh clothes again. He had stopped crying by this time, although still looked very suspicious, but cheered up during the next stage of the ceremony when he was carried around the sacred table three times by the godfather, with Papa Andreas solemnly leading the way.

It was all over soon after that and we found our way back to the parents' house where we were introduced to a little old lady who turned out to be the child's great grandmother and had once lived in Wales. When we left a couple of hours later we drove Papa Yanni back to his village before returning to our little dark house by the stream.

The baptism had taken place on a Saturday and the following morning we were woken by the earnest insistent chanting of Papa Andreas in the same church and the little taciturn man who sings mass with him. There are loudspeakers high up in the church's blue dome so that the whole village can hear the service but the abrupt side of the valley opposite our house amplifies the sound naturally for us anyway.

As I lay there listening to Papa Andreas' strong baritone voice I thought about the naked slippery child he had held high the day before and wondered briefly what he would be in life when he grew up. There was no doubt in my mind that, at the very least, after his long ordeal in the crowded church at such a tender age, he would never be able to forget that he was a Greek.

CHAPTER SEVEN

*I*T WAS DECEMBER NOW AND THE SKY WAS BRIGHT again although I couldn't understand at first what people meant when they nodded sagely and said that the sun was showing its teeth. I noticed that Papa Philippos had started sawing up the huge pile of thick olive branches outside his house and then Nico began waxing quite lyrical about the deep pleasure of sitting in front of log fires with a glass of raki in his hand. He hadn't struck me as naturally suited to a cardigan and slippers before and I began to realise that cold days in the valley were around the corner even though it still felt quite warm to me.

We had bought a cast iron stove in the flea market at Athens a couple of months earlier and Antonis had said he would install it for us and clamp the pipes to the outside wall when he had time. It wasn't exactly a sure sign of changing weather when he suddenly decided to do it half way through the month but his timing was immaculate. The temperature had already started dropping when I found myself half way up a ladder trying to hold a steel band around the stovepipe in place against the wall. I don't know how cold it was on the cement roof where Antonis lay on his belly with a hammer in one hand and nails in the other but he was shivering when we finished and demanded a cup of hot coffee.

It turned really cold the next day and I didn't need any further persuading that snow was lurking somewhere over the mountains when Nico appeared on one of his mules wearing an old leather hat with flaps over his ears. He had brought more wood and was clearly impressed by the heat generated from the stove, which Antonis had lit using woodshavings from a wall cupboard he had restored for us and some of the smaller logs. The wall cupboard had been left in the house by the old lady whose son we had bought it from but had almost been falling to pieces before Antonis had worked his magic on it.

I still couldn't quite believe how he had turned the battered old piece of furniture into the handsome cabinet now hanging in the corner opposite the kitchen, even though I had watched him perform the trick. It would have been an impressive achievement for a cabinet maker with all the right tools for the job but Antonis had worked only with what happened to be lying around the house, apart from the new panes of glass for the broken doors which we had brought from the local hardware store. He had fixed it about four feet above the floor in a corner of the room between two windows by first of all filing a long iron bolt in two and then hammering each rod into the stone walls to provide firm supports. A couple of strong nails through each side of the cupboard into the walls as well and there it was propped nicely in the angle above a white stone shelf waiting for Antonis to start blowing on his fingers.

It still looked in a pretty sorry state at that stage of course, with one of its three shelves partly eaten away like an old dry sandwich, and missing one of the long triangular pieces of wood on either side to make it seem flush against the angled walls. I think it was a carpenter's adze that Antonis used to repair these deficiencies and he spent one careful morning delicately shaping two pieces of derelict wood to fill in the spaces. When he fitted them to the beautiful ruined cupboard they looked like clumsy forgeries until he got to work with brush and a pot of dark varnish. After he had finished the structure gleamed as richly as any antique cabinet and he had even managed to find an old swivel catch for the doors that looked as though it had been especially made for it.

I had realised long before this that the way to seriously involve Antonis in projects was to attempt them myself and then wait for his natural impatience to take over. This is what I did when I started digging the garden shortly after he had got the stove working for the first time and was sawing some wood on the terrace. After watching me incredulously for a few minutes he took hold of a pickaxe and showed me how it should be done. An hour later the large oblong patch of earth I had chosen in front of three lemon trees was looking like an enormous bar of pleated chocolate and he was planting broad beans and garlic cloves.

It was clearly going to snow before very long but Marylle and I were leaving the island in the morning to spend Christmas with friends near Athens and I tried to imagine how the valley would look when it came. The plane trees were fierce grey skeletons now, of course, but the olive trees were still preening themselves under a brilliant sky and bright oranges hung from a thousand trees. It didn't feel at all like winter and, when Antonis lit a fire in the front room, it was as though he had smuggled flames from the sun into the house.

When we returned a week later there was snow on the high ground everywhere in Greece and the weather had been so rough the day before that no boats had been allowed to leave harbour. It was a grave and peaceful afternoon when we caught the ferry from Rafina, however, with a misty sea only marginally lighter in shade than the swollen grey-blue sky hanging over it, and not a snowflake in sight. There were children running excitedly about the ferry as it glided solemnly past the snow-capped mountains of Evia and festive lights hung from trees in dark gardens as we drove through the quiet villages of Andros a couple of hours later.

It was almost the last day of the year now and the merry kids on the boat had been winding themselves up for their second treat in a week. The idea of giving presents on Christmas Day has only caught on in Greece during recent years and, traditionally, these annual rewards for good behaviour have always been delivered in the early hours of New Year's Day by a reverend gentleman known as Saint Vassilis. I don't imagine any but the very youngest kids believe in this supposed nocturnal benefactor any more than Santa Claus but it doesn't stop them expecting two lots of seasonal goodies within a few days of each other.

They also get to make a spirited commotion in the streets on New Year's Eve since this is the day they are allowed to visit houses in their neighbourhood and sing for pennies. It is a custom which has obvious affinities with carol singing, but I had never witnessed it in the suburb of Athens where we had lived before and learned about it only when we were woken up in the Chora house the following morning by an incredible racket. When I stumbled out of bed to investigate, I was confronted with a little girl wrapped up in a warm coat and scarf beating lustily on a tin drum and an even smaller boy with a triangle.

They stopped to stare up at me in my dressing gown and I turned to Marylle who was standing at my shoulder smiling foolishly down at them.

— What do they want?

— They're waiting for you to ask them to sing.

— For money, I suppose.

— Of course.

The two tiny minstrels had been following our exchange with puzzled frowns on their faces but took it as a signal to start their caterwauling when I nodded at this. It was only when the boy opened his mouth to reach for a high note that his overcoat parted as well and a long loaf of bread he was obviously taking back home popped into view. I was reminded at once of a story my mother tells about me during the second world war when I was found singing carols with a bottle of beer I had been sent out to buy for Christmas lunch under my arm. There is nothing so moving as bright reminders of one's own childhood, of course, and the kids looked at me with astonishment when I presented them with a bank note instead of the coins they had been expecting.

I had fallen asleep the night before thinking about the lights in trees we had seen driving from the ferry and there were more strung from plane trees in the square when we went out into the main street. There is an old peoples' home behind it which was a gift from one of the wealthy shipping families and several of its ancient residents were scowling at other eager children in the square banging away at their instruments.

There was celebration in the air but I didn't expect to be offered nuts and sweet cakes with brandy and water when we popped into the bank to draw out some money. Apparently this is customary in the island on the last day of the year but I was accustomed to the hushed respect which attends these transactions in England and was taken aback for a few moments.

(On reflection I shouldn't have been, for I had walked past a bank outside Athens early one evening about three months earlier and seen wild gaiety in its cold windows. When I peered inside I realised there was a small party taking place and excited female cashiers were being waltzed around between wall safes and steel filing cabinets. I approved of this when I thought about it but my first reaction on witnessing such behaviour in a hall of money was that it was as heretical as swilling champagne in a Methodist chapel.)

We were going to fill some bottles with spring water after

– 96 –

seeing what further work Antonis had done in the valley house although we wouldn't be meeting him until that evening. The Greeks mark the turning of each year by playing cards at midnight, which I suppose makes sense as a tradition given that life has usually been a gamble for most of them, and we were going to eat at the hotel in Apikia where he would be playing the violin.

A couple of motionless old men were sitting outside the café bar as we drove up to the valley and I noticed a single pink cyclamen growing in the roots of an olive tree when I got out of the car. I had a coffee before walking down the steps to where the house was gleaming in the winter sunshine. There were stiff red pomegranates hanging from a leafless tree in our neighbour's garden but most of their flesh had been eaten by birds.

Of course not a lot had been done in the house in the short time we had been away but we were still pleased to find a wooden cabinet for holding plates hanging proudly from a wall in the kitchen. While Marylle busied herself dusting I went into the garden and stood there admiring the trees and tidy stretches of earth around me. I had worked hard weeding the garden and Nico had planted it with the seeds of a cereal that could be dug back into the soil in Spring to form a natural green manure.

After a while Marylle came down to join me and we walked down to stand on our favourite rocky station looking at the busy stream. I was quite proud of this little site because, although it had been covered with brushwood and leafmould three months earlier, I had sensed that there was something massive and special beneath. After clearing everything away I had found a platform of large and beautifully curved boulders sloping down towards the water.

The plan now was to build a stone table in the middle of them together with a stone bench.

From where we stood at that moment we could see that,

7 ROBERT LEIGH, *Sunlight in the wine*

despite the boisterous rampaging of the water, there was a natural pool formed by rocks and intertwined branches just below the bank to our left which had a relatively calm surface.

I could imagine myself sitting there late in the day with glass in hand some time in the future and turned to Marylle.

— I might try and make a little Japanese water garden there later in the year.

— With water lilies you mean?

— That's right. We could even have some floating oil lamps in the water when evening falls.

She smiled at the idea although I could see she thought I was being fanciful.

— I like the idea of the lilies anyway. We'd better go and get the spring water now though.

I don't know how many springs there are in Andros but I'm sure Marylle will get to know every single one of them before our time is up among living people. She has a passion for the natural waters of the earth that rivals any studied ardour for wines. I had been told by Spaniards from the hills and valleys below Granada that no spring water is the same but I hadn't realised before I met Marylle how differently they can taste.

It was obvious when I thought about it, of course, because the springs are in different parts of the island and each takes body and flavour from the various concentrations of minerals in its locality. There are some that are as frisky as champagne, and others which slide into the glass with a stately fluidity that reminds me of a mature white wine. They are those kinds of solemn liquids which never leave an obvious taste in the mouth but deposit their flavour nicely in the kidneys after a suitable period of time. I love them all and can get high on either water or beverage if the sun makes its presence clear in the glass.

The spring we were going to milk for its water now was up a steep path not far from where Antonis lives and was new to both Marylle and me. It was a ten minute climb up huge stone steps and then along the edge of a small escarpment with trees growing at right angles from it. We heard the water before turning a corner in the path and then saw it trickling down from the high rocks above in about a dozen different places. The main body of water was piped down into a sort of wide stone font and we tasted it before filling up our various flagons and bottles. It rested fatly in the mouth but left a slightly tart smack on the tongue after swallowing it.

It was late afternoon now and we stopped to admire two great high rocks silhouetted against the dying sun with a row of grey beehives perched on top of them. Down in the village again we popped into the cafe bar and ran into Papa Philippos in a plaid shirt and black cardigan. There was a glass on the table in front of him and he shrugged at me when I sat down next to him and asked for a Greek coffee with a little brandy in it.

— What can you do? I know the doctors told me not to drink but it's New Year's Eve.

— It's your life but you're taking a chance.

There was a scowl on his bearded face as he reached for the glass and drank the contents.

— I'm sure God doesn't mind.

It was my turn to shrug as I savoured the brandy in my bitter black coffee.

— He doesn't have to worry about having only two kidneys.

I don't know whether he thought this was blasphemous or not, although I've never heard people blaspheme so much as the Spaniards and the Greeks, but two teenagers came up with a pack of cards at that moment and he turned his attention to them.

It was about half an hour before midnight when we finally arrived at the hotel where there were about thirty people in the lounge and a huge round log burning in the fireplace. A number of them were playing cards already but Antonis and his wife were warming themselves near the fire. I ordered drinks and the young woman who staggered up with them was clearly not only foreign but on the way to being drunk. Later I found out that she was Swiss and that her new husband had been killed in a car accident while driving in Greece on their honeymoon. She was paying her way by working at the hotel and told us without much conviction that she was saving up to travel home again.

Antonis asked whether we wanted to join him for cards with other guests at a green table but we didn't know the game and sat chewing tiny sweet cakes until midnight. There was a commotion of intimacy when the hotel manager declared the hour was upon us and everybody started kissing each other on both cheeks and wishing many years on earth. Armoured clumsily in my Protestant skin, however, I just grinned idiotically at people and even felt a little embarrassed at kissing the delightful Marylle in front of them.

Five minutes later we found ourselves in a queue waiting to greet a bright-eyed old lady with dumpling cheeks and a rigorous coiffeur who was standing by the reception desk. I hadn't the slightest idea who she was and hardly noticed the thoroughly erect consort standing by her side until she leaned forward to be kissed by me. It was the hotel manager who told us afterwards that she was 84, her proud husband 88, and that they had been coming to the hotel every New Year's Eve since it opened to celebrate her birthday, which was, of course, on the first day of each new year.

After paying our respects to this lively octogenarian we sat down for our meal, waited in vain afterwards for Antonis to start playing his violin, and then left in the early hours of a wintry night. As we drove down towards a black and ominous sea we saw snow whirling in the harbour lights and were glad we were spending the night at Chora. There was a genuine snowstorm in the windows the next morning and it wasn't until the day after that I drove gingerly up to the valley and parked outside the café bar.

There was no snow down near the house, although it lay

like white stubble across the expanse of mountain in the distance, but the stream sounded as though it was full of flashing icicles. The sheer extraordinary coldness of the weather on an island that had been hot for so long called to mind an article I had just read about a similar catastrophic fall of temperature in Provence. The writer had described olive trees shrieking in agony as the sap froze in them during the night but I heard no sound from the trees across the stream apart from the wind moaning hoarsely through their naked branches.

While there, we collected some logs from our wood cellar to take back to Chora and hauled them up to the car in black rubber tool bags. I hadn't expected the café bar to be open but Nico was sitting inside with his brother the priest and an older man I didn't know with the face of an intelligent walnut. It was cold in the bar and Nico was wearing his black cap with the ear flaps while the other man had a woolly bobble hat above eyebrows that were crinkled up like old blue scars and a thick grey sweater.

After a while it emerged that he lived on his own in an ancient house farther down the valley that I remembered walking past once and noticing a line of stiff shirts and long underpants drying in the garden. He was a chatty old bird who told us that he was retired but used to live down in Chora during the war where he had a jeweller's shop.

The German Commandant had appeared one day with a diamond that had fallen out of a brooch he wanted repaired.

— I hope he paid for the work.

The eyebrows lifted again and the wrinkled face seemed to spin with amusement.

— I got a special price it.

— What was that?

— There was a shortage of food at that time and I asked him for a sack of potatoes. They were delivered to the shop as soon as I had finished.

— What were the Germans like?

— They seemed all right to me. I think most of them were home sick.

One of the owners of the café bar came across with some bowls of steaming soup but Nico shook his head when I asked if he wanted some.

— I'm supposed to be home to eat in a few minutes but the wife is busy. Both the kids are in bed with flu.

— I'm sorry to hear that. It can't be much fun working on your own.

When he made a face and shrugged the old leather cap around his head appeared to stop his scowl from spreading all around the café.

— There's nothing much for them to do in this weather anyway. They stay indoors most of the time.

— What about you?

— I'm up after dawn as usual. Somebody has to look after the animals.

Although it was still extremely cold a couple of days later we decided to brave it and spent the night in the house. We planned to put in electric radiators but our only source of heating at that time was wood fires and I quickly got one going in the front room. After eating homemade pizza topped with fresh tomato sauce and drinking wine from Vourkoti we sat hypnotised by the crackling logs while I drank some of Nico's raki.

It reminded me of the coal fire in the parlour of the council house where I grew up in Kent, of chilblains suffered from sitting next to it after coming in from a chaos of snow outside, and then of muffins toasted over its embers on beautiful long brass forks. When we retired to sleep it also brought back memories of how cold that house could be in winter, since the warmth of the fire didn't reach into the bedroom and we exchanged startled shouts at the icy touch of the sheets.

When Nico popped in for a coffee the following morning he asked if we wanted Papa Andreas to sprinkle the rooms in the house with holy water after he had blessed it on Epiphany. This is when all water in Greece, including the sea itself, is blessed by a priest and Nico, who has a great instinct for getting as much as possible out of every ritual, told us he always takes some of this blessed water after the church service to sprinkle on his land.

Of course we wanted our house blessed but, in the event, we weren't there in time for Papa Andreas because we went down to see the ceremony of the holy cross being tossed into the sea and missed him by minutes.

It seemed to me that the cross was raised above the water in a particularly spectacular and hazardous manner that day. The weather was still terrible and the priest in his splendid green and gold robe needed three straining men to hold him by its skirts as he balanced on wet rocks over a green and raging sea with the crucifix held high before him.

This is getting ahead of things, however, because he was the priest of a large church in Chora near the sea with a history that says much about Andros and the ingrained convictions of its people. According to the priest it was built early in the sixteenth century but, at the last moment, funds ran out before a roof could be put on. There matters rested, with the structure open to the elements, until there was a violent storm one day and, when it finally subsided, enough ships' timbers were found on the beach to make an extremely handsome roof.

The islanders were convinced that this had been a miracle and I didn't feel at all cynical when I heard the story, for surely, if miracles are going to come from anywhere, it must be the nearest sea.

CHAPTER EIGHT

*T*HE MEMORY OF THE PRIEST IN HIS GREEN AND GOLD vestments leaning out over the dripping rocks stayed in my mind as the ferry bucked in a way that clearly alarmed the lorry drivers travelling with us. We had stayed on the island a further week but then had to return to Athens before visiting my mother at the old people's home where she lives in Yorkshire now. I was glad we had spent those few extra days in our village, however, if only because Nico's son Yanni had introduced us to an explosive drink the local people take on winter evenings. This is some raki mixed with honey and, when heated on a fire or stove, is a beverage guaranteed to raise the body temperature excitingly and produce interesting whistling sounds in each ear.

There had been little change in the weather and I was mildly surprised that we could even get to the mainland that particular afternoon. The wind had not been too bad earlier as the ferry had been slipping down from the islands of Mykonos and Tinos, but it was beginning to turn very nasty as we waited to drive on board. It was clear that it was going to be a rough ride and when the ferry moved away from the lee of the island into a stretch of open water foaming waves appeared in the windows as it pitched and rolled.

I wasn't really alarmed when one of the ship's officers said it was a force eight gale, although this is the outside limit at which ferries are allowed to sail, and my surprise at the lorry drivers' consternation went away when I realised that most were from the mainland. The island Greeks grow up with the sea all around them, of course, and many have spent a part of their working lives as sailors. The sea is one of the dimensions which shape the way they live and they treat it almost as a kind of collective mother, to be respected but not really feared, because, after all, it is the vast open womb from which life itself, and all possible reassurance about the strange experience of living, comes.

This may sound mystical and romantic but I am convinced most of my island friends feel this as a truth in their blood. It certainly must be true that their ancestors learned to rely on the sea in a way they never could on a life ashore which was always subject to the whims and caprices of those who occupied the country. The sea may be cruel sometimes but it doesn't discriminate against any particular race and nobody has ever owned it. This alone must sometimes make it a more congenial environment than the land and probably accounts for the tremendous success the Greeks have always had in the shipping industry.

I don't know whether the ancient need to placate the elements is at the root of the ceremony of blessing the waters, although I would be surprised if it wasn't. The priests say that it celebrates Christ's baptism but the ceremony is attended by so much theatre and passion that it must surely satisfy other immemorial feelings. It is the priest who throws the cross into the sea but an icon showing the holy baptism is always shown to the waves by local fishermen, who clearly need to believe in God's power over all the elements.

When Marylle and I had watched the ceremony a week earlier the weather couldn't have been more unpleasant but it hadn't stopped the local dignitaries and a long line of celebrants turning out with the priest. The village band was in the procession and, when the priest in his glowing robes stepped up to balance precariously on the rocks, it was the harbourmaster among others who held grimly on to his billowing skirts.

I had seen pictures before of the ceremony on television as it used to be performed and it had usually involved eager young men diving into the water to rescue the cross. This custom is no longer practised but, in any event, the sea was really violent this time, with raging mists of spray blowing across it and great white waves careering towards the shore. The idea of anyone trying to recover a crucifix from its depths was out of the question and the priest had tied a cord to the cross he carried so that he could pull it out again.

The wind made even this stratagem difficult and he had to hurl it away from him three times before it cleared the rocks and sank beneath the exploding waves. I had never met this particular priest before but he made an impressive figure up there on the rocks. He must have been nearly seventy, with his fine white hair tied in a small bun on the back of his neck, and, although there was charged activity all around him, not a flicker of alarm worried his face as he hauled in the crucifix with the dignitaries clinging to his robe.

When the ceremony was over he stepped calmly down from the rocks and headed away back to his church with the wet cross held out in front of him. After the church had emptied later we spoke to him and he confirmed the story about the wood for the roof appearing miraculously on the shore and also showed us an icon which is apparently quite famous.

— Melina Mercouri wanted to have it in an Athens museum, he said. She was the Minister of Culture in the socialist government at the time.

— What happened?

— We didn't let her have it, he said. Everybody knows it belongs in this church.

I have read travel books which say that Andros is one of those islands with an interior in which you can forget the sea but I don't think the writers can have talked to the inhabitants. It is true that it is not an island of the kind that Henry Miller described as being a marriage of rocks and sky, where everything about it declares that it had just been heaved out of the sea, but there are tiny shells to be found even in the deep valleys and the sea is reflected in the sky. Whenever the olive trees rustle people know that 'sheep are beginning to leap around' out towards the white horizon.

I don't think I know any man in our village who hasn't been a sailor at some time, or, despite the fact that the shipping industry is in the doldrums and shipowners tend to use Philippine crews nowadays, any boy who doesn't suppose that he might have to learn the ways of the sea in the years to come. Although I knew that Antonis had been chief cook on a merchant ship and that Nico had been a sailor for a number of years, I didn't know that his tough bearded brother had been a second cook before putting on the cloth.

It was clear that Papa Andreas must have held a position of some authority on his ship, although he hadn't been an officer, and I was reassured to learn that he had been the helmsman, since that is a role that fits his character perfectly. I find it difficult to imagine him sitting down with Papa Leonidas and Papa Philippos to discuss ecclesiastical matters but, if this ever happened, I am sure they would get around sooner or later to swapping stories of life at sea.

After a while it began to dawn on me that people on the island regarded the sea as the nearest source of employment until recently, much as the men on the estate where I grew up regarded the paper mill at the bottom of the street, and that it didn't hold that much more romance for them. This was a disappointment to me at first because I wanted to imagine bold young men running away to sea in search of adventure and old sea salts with tales to stir the blood. The fact that working as a sailor might have taken them to the other ends of the earth seemed beside the point for most of the islanders. It was simply the most available way of saving up some money before they returned to their villages and settled down. But the shipping slump has taken even this possibility away from them now and, unfortunately, many of the younger men are having to seek work on the mainland.

One of the few men I knew in our village who had made a career out of being a sailor, until he was in his fifties at least, was Leonidas, the elder brother of Nico and Papa Philippos, who was chief steward on oil tankers until he retired a couple of years ago. I dare say he must have looked resplendent in his uniform then but when I see him nowadays he is trudging past our house in his old clothes with tools over his shoulder. He is on the way to work his land like any other man in the village and the fact that he has spent so long at sea doesn't seem to mean that he has fewer skills than them. He was another one of the men who worked with the old mason Yorgo when he was putting the new roof on the house, and turned up recently with Antonis to build a cement conduit which now takes water from the communal channel into our garden. He is clearly competent at most of the crafts necessary to survive as an islander, including seamanship, which I suppose must have been true for pretty well every man on Andros at one time.

The sea has also been the heaving route which Greeks have travelled many times to escape oppression or seek new economic opportunities when times have been bad in their own country. There was a substantial migration in the last century from the Aegean islands to Egypt, for instance, where there were apparently over 100,000 Greeks living by the time the first world war broke out. It is also an astonishing fact that almost one quarter of Greek men under forty emigrated to the United

States during the first fifteen years of this century and that, subject to immigration restrictions, many more have done so since then.

A number of young men from Andros were on these sad pilgrimages and those who returned had usually spent a long time abroad. One of the results of this nowadays is that the island is relatively sophisticated, in the sense that many of its inhabitants have experience of the outside world as either sailors or migrants, although it has none of the surface glitter and nonsense that word usually implies. The island doesn't put out a huge welcome mat for visitors but there is scarcely a man who doesn't have a few words of English or, even, Spanish, which seems the other main language heard at sea.

It was because I can stumble around in Spanish that I became friendly with the owner of a café bar in Chora the first time I came to the island with Marylle. She hadn't been divorced long at that time and was shy about being seen with me in public so I trotted away to have a coffee by myself.

As I walked into the bar a Greek basketball team had just lost a crucial match in Barcelona and the owner swore in Spanish at the television set before asking me what I wanted to drink.

— Un cafe con cognac, por favor.

He frowned at me.

— Are you Spanish?

— I'm English as it happens but I don't speak much Greek. Did you learn Spanish at school?

The frown melted as he shook his head.

— I picked it up when I was at sea. The ship I was on called in at several Spanish ports regularly.

We were talking about various parts of Spain that we both knew when another customer walked in and stood listening to us. I could see that he was impressed by the owner's linguistic ability and my new friend winked at me as he turned away to talk to him. When I asked for my bill later he refused to accept any money and slapped me on the back as I walked out.

— Hasta la vista amigo.

The first people we met in the village who had spent some years abroad were Dimitris, the tenant of the café bar at the top of the steps before he went back to Athens, and his wife and daughters. He had worked as a chef in a restaurant while his daughters were at school in New York and returned to Greece when they were teenagers. I imagine he must have spent most of his time there with his fellow expatriates because his English was almost as primitive as my Greek and he spoke it with great reluctance.

He was as moody as chefs are always alleged to be and there were times when he would suddenly rush across the café to embrace me while shouting like some new immigrant in a bad American movie.

— Hallo my friend Bobby. What you been doing today?

(I had told him once that the only person allowed to call me by that diminutive was my mother but he paid no more attention to this than he did to what I ordered. If he wanted to serve me some taramasalata he would do so no matter what wistful thoughts my stomach might be entertaining.)

He was a good cook and one of his regular customers was a stocky grey-haired man who was presumably a competent judge because he had once owned four Greek restaurants in New York. A man in his sixties, he had the build of an old bull and was the father of two sons who were bulky enough to challenge his authority but were patently still in awe of him. I always imagined that they must have lived in some New York tenement crowded with other immigrants because, whenever they were together, they communicated with a kind of affectionate roaring, as though they were accustomed to having to drown out other competing noises in order to establish contact with each other.

This certainly happened whenever the two sons turned up by themselves, which was usually on the same fragile motor scooter driven by the larger one. He was about five years older than his brother and they bawled at each other fondly in a language they must have developed on the chaotic streets of Brooklyn. I didn't understand why they did this in the middle of a quiet Greek village until I remembered that my sister's two sons, who live in Spain with her, used to speak to each other in the local dialect when they didn't want her to understand. It seemed a reasonable guess that the two Greek brothers had acquired the same habit when younger in order to tell each other secrets.

Whatever the reason, they would roar away to each other in an extraordinary idiom that bore only a marginal relationship to ordinary demotic American and was freighted with the kind of emphatic swear words only small boys delight in using all the time. There was no doubt that it was their own private language because they would change to Greek immediately when talking to other customers and even to a halting English with me.

It was the father who fascinated me the most, however, not only because he spoke as though trying to shout through sandpaper, but because of the obvious respect in which he was held by his large sons. It was the same mixture of healthy caution and admiration that Nico's boys had for him and probably for the same reason. I imagine that both men had demanded a good deal from their sons before they were allowed to think of themselves as adults and a father can only get away with this if he sets an example in his own life.

There were many differences in character between the two fathers but both had a stubborn and pugnacious attitude towards life as well as the energy to work incredibly hard. They had set their faces to the wind and took a pride in their willpower and strength, which had clearly helped shape the way their sons felt about things. This seems to me more likely to happen in communities where respect is earned by the degree of commitment shown to common purposes than by constantly chasing one's own tail in order to be different.

I can easily visualise the young bull from Andros arriving at Staten Island and rolling up his sleeves as he prepared to start work immediately. I don't know how long it took him to acquire his four restaurants but I'm sure he carried his sense of community with him and always had it in mind that he would return to his island one day.

He also had a feeling for those down on their luck, which used to be common among Mediterranean people, and arose from their shared sense that life is always uncertain and misfortune can happen to anyone. Since he was also protective towards the opposite sex he must have been a godsend to the pretty woman he told me about who turned up at his restaurant one day and then didn't have enough money to pay the bill.

— I never give handouts to bums, he said, but I could see she was fine woman in trouble so I told her to forget it and gave her free coffee as well.

— She must have been grateful.

He nodded with satisfaction.

— She ate at my place many times and we became good friends.

Although I had said nothing, he looked up at me with sudden alarm.

— There wasn't no hanky panky about it, he said fiercely. She was just beautiful woman down on her luck and I was happy to help her.

— Of course.

There were lively memories in his eyes now and he frowned as he put down his coffee.

— I tried to give her money but she wouldn't take it.

— She must have had her pride then.

— I told you she was one god-damned fine woman. The most beautiful lady I knew in my whole life.

— Do you know what happened to her?

He looked around the café bar before leaning across the table and staring at me dramatically.

— If I told you her name you would not believe me. She's famous actress in movies now and I helped her when she was in trouble. What do you think of that for something in my god-damned life?

I was hoping he was going to tell me the name of this radiant creature but he only sat back and folded his arms so I just nodded at him in what I hoped was an understanding manner.

— I suppose we never know who we are going to meet. It can be a funny life one way and the other.

He scowled as some other memory stirred in him.

— Sometimes it's not so god-damned funny either.

I assume most of the sea captains speak some English but we don't meet them very often. When I spoke to one who lives just outside our village he said that there had been several hundred captains from Andros at one time and, if this is true, it means that around five per cent of the island's population had been qualified to command a ship. Nowadays many live near Athens but some have houses in the village above the great ruined water mill which Marylle had once hoped could be turned into a rare music palace. It always puzzled me why they wanted to build houses there since it is not an easy village to find and, as far as I have been able to determine, had only one café bar in the entire place until recently.

It is a very handsome village, however, and the houses have a decorative solidity which I suppose, must have appealed to men who spent much of their lives at sea dreaming of a place where the floorboards don't creak, the bed is always warm, and there are roses outside the front door. The fact that it lies off the beaten track makes sense of a kind as well, since the women were hidden away from easy view and, if strangers did appear, could band together quickly at the first sign of aggravation. There is presumably nothing like a history of raids by heterosexual pirates to encourage both a sense of privacy and of a desperate neighbourliness when necessary.

I hadn't been in Andros long before we had urgent need of

one of these captains to take a boy to a hospital on the mainland late one evening. He was the captain of a ferry who was at home in the village for the night when he was called out by the police after consultation with doctors working in the island medical clinic. The boy was in a party with a German friend of ours and, in trying to protect his head when falling from the top of the ruined Venetian castle at Chora, had broken both his arms very badly.

It was only when he had been transferred to the ferry and it had left for the mainland with Marylle along to translate that I realised there were no other passengers. I have heard many criticisms of Greek medical facilities but the absence of transport from the islands in an emergency cannot be one of them. The entire ferry, complete with captain and crew, had been commandeered for the sake of one German lad who was in danger of being crippled for life.

(As it happened, his injuries were so bad that, following one night in a Greek hospital, he had to be put on a plane back to Germany where there were more advanced facilities. A couple of years later the boy turned up on the island to thank people for their help, and told me that he had started playing tennis once more, although at one time it had been thought that he would never lift a racquet again).

It appears that not all sea captains return from their voyages to comfortable village houses with eager families waiting for them. I was surprised by how large the clinic the boy had been taken to was for a small island but was talking to an old man not long ago who said that the cost of the building itself had been met from the estate of a sea captain. Apparently, the captain had neither wife nor family when he died and left money for the erection of the clinic in his will.

The only captain I know well myself retired some years ago but still looks as though he could dance a stately jig if he felt the urge come upon him. I thought he was in his early sixties when we first met and was astonished when he told me diffidently that he was almost eighty. He said nothing when I asked what his secret was, but he doesn't seem to worry about anything, gives the impression that he has never felt the need to rush anywhere in his life, and swims about a quarter of a mile most summer days with a solemn breast stroke and an erect head that stares directly ahead of him.

I have been in stormy situations a couple of times where I felt that the sea was prepared to swallow the entire ship just to get at me but I don't think I would have worried if he had been the captain. He is clearly destined for a long life, speaks English with calm authority, and is so disciplined it is sometimes difficult to believe he is Greek.

He looks absurdly healthy as he strolls around Chora and smiled with pleasure one day when I greeted him as I would a young man. There are a lot of kilometres in his head though, as the Spaniards say, and he clearly feels them sometimes because the next time I saluted him in the same way he frowned a little testily.

— Stop that nonsense Bob, he said. I don't feel like a young man at all these days.

CHAPTER NINE

*H*OWEVER OLD THE CAPTAIN FEELS, HE IS STILL walking around, but my mother, who is only six years older, can hardly get out of bed nowadays. She has osteoporosis, which is said to be a normal disorder of the aging process that can be brought on by prolonged inactivity. This can't be true of my mother, who has worked hard all her life, and is much more likely to have been caused by a poor diet, due, until she was in her fifties at least, to poverty and a stubborn refusal to spend money on herself.

I know she would have loved the little green valley on the island but I could only show her photographs of it and try to amuse her with little anecdotes about life there. We spent a fortnight with her but then had to go down to London where I had a couple of appointments and Marylle was meeting some friends from Andros. When we had dinner with a couple one evening who work for a shipping company the conversation was mostly about the island.

Although the shipping industry is no longer the force it once was on Andros, there are still many people from the island who earn their living from it one way or another. Most of them live on the mainland now but always spend their summer holidays on the island and speak perfectly adequate English. There are also a few others who appear from some of the more privileged enclaves in Europe speaking it with the kind of elegant fluency that only comes with an expensive international education. They are children of the island but were born into shipping families who could afford to live where the darker tides of history wouldn't touch them too much.

The couple we know devote themselves primarily to classical pursuits but the new generation of shipowners appear to be too busy making their fortunes to bother about that sort of thing. As it happens, the most powerful shipping clan from Andros has a couple of members who have established, not just an archeological museum, which might have been expected, but two handsome modern art museums which wouldn't disgrace a small gilded metropolis.

(There is something absurd but immensely pleasurable in climbing out of a frothing sea on a Greek island, drinking ouzo with cheese and olives under a plane tree, and then ambling into hushed and air-conditioned marble salons to see a Picasso or Paul Klee exhibition).

It is difficult to imagine anything else that could demonstrate quite so eloquently the extraordinary wealth that some of the inhabitants of this island have managed to accumulate but perhaps it has always been thus. I was reading not long ago that the husband of the great classical woman poet Sappho had been a rich merchant from Andros.

Of course most people on the island are more interested in their own customs than what the pundits might think is high art and there are activities which owe nothing to outside influences. Marylle and I have often promised each other to learn the intricate island dances after watching exhibitions of them by local children and many Andros women are still skilled at the traditional lacecraft for which the island was once renowned.

I gather that Andros was a considerable centre of learning in mediaeval times and, if it ever reaches such heights again, it will be due in no small part to another shipowner, who is a Byzantine scholar and someone who identifies himself passionately with Andros. It was because of his enthusiastic lobbying of other shipping people that a magnificent library has been collected and installed in a beautiful old house in Chora, and illustrated books commissioned on aspects of the island's history.

A great friend of Marylle works in this library and I understand from her that there are plans for other books on the island's customs and traditions. It is apparently hoped to include a collection of recipes handed down through the generations and, after reading in James Bent about cakes made with honey and walnuts and served on lemon leaves, not to mention jam from lemon flowers and roses, I shall be first in the bookshop when it is published.

The most vital and pervasive expression of any culture is its music, I imagine, and Greece probably has more choirs than Wales. Andros is no exception and not long ago Marylle and I attended one of its sessions in a draughty building sometimes used by the local school. They were rehearsing their entry for an international choir festival in Athens later that month under the baton of a man with a round pleading face who teaches piano to some of the island children.

Their musical selection was varied for such an event and they finished the proceedings with a famous Russian lament of great movement and passion. I knew most of the male singers but there was one quiet little man in the corner I hadn't met before and it was he who suddenly launched into a refrain with a powerful tenor voice that made the hairs on the back of my neck stand on end. I happen to have a passion for opera and those hairs expect to come to attention quite often, but the only time before this they had been similarly startled was in a pub near the Welsh border some twenty five years ago. It was after midnight, the police had gone to bed, and the entire clientele were singing drunkenly except one little man in the corner who appeared to have gone to sleep. The song was a beautiful Welsh anthem called 'David of the White Rock' and it was this quiet sozzled creature who suddenly came erect and sang in a voice like a bugle in the forest until everyone else fell silent.

Since Marylle and I had sat through the rehearsal, we felt it almost a duty to go to the real thing, so we turned up at the choir festival a couple of weeks later in a booming old Athens concert hall. There were choirs from Amsterdam to Kiev, including one from the Ukraine which sounded like a perfect choral expression of the socialist dream, and another composed of solemn schoolgirls from Salonika. I don't know what it says about me but when the girls sang the English phrase 'Trust in the Lord' from a song by Felix Mendelssohn there were tears in my eyes.

Although I suppose a lot of people in the hall were friends and relatives of the singers, it was still full every day of the festival, but then many Greek people seem to have an almost desperate hunger for the kind of rich creative experiences they missed out on for centuries. A couple of years ago Marylle and I saw Shakespeare's last three plays directed by Peter Hall at the great open amphitheatre of Epidavros, which was built for the patients of an ancient healing site between cooling pine trees and low hills. There wasn't a seat free for any of the performances, and yet the beautiful site is in the open countryside at least three hours drive from Athens, while the language of those marvellous plays requires close attention even from an Englishman who knows them.

There was a lot of competition from the other choirs of course, but, when the judging was finally over, the Andros choir had been awarded ninth place, which we thought was a marvellous achievement for what is largely a collection of musical shopkeepers from a comparatively small island.

The first time I swam in Andros was from a tiny little beach and the way into the sea was through narrow channels of sand between great broken tongues of flat stone. We had arrived on the ferry only half an hour earlier and, as I picked my way along these rivulets of sand, I looked up to see it moving down towards its next stop at Tinos in the water ahead of me. There was a group of small bare islands just behind it and seagulls rose wildly above them at the sound of the ferry's foghorn.

These islands are part of Andros and a year later I found myself on the largest one, picking up cuttlefish bones discarded by the seagulls with the magnificent yacht we had just left parked on the shining water nearer the shore. The yacht belonged to the family of one of Marylle's friends and we were exploring the little islands before joining other guests on it for dinner.

The white-haired American lady in a pink jump suit I sat next to during the meal seemed sweetness itself but told me that she had been a crime reporter on an American daily newspaper before her marriage with a reputation for her toughness. She had clearly mellowed considerably since then and spent much of the meal telling me about her wonderful Irish butler, who had apparently been her strength and consolation after her husband had died, and was at that moment on holiday in Galway while she was being entertained in Greece. It seemed that her late husband had been a prominent businessman and she had inherited the controlling stock in the company he had founded, although she confessed that she didn't really understand most of the products it made. I gathered later that it was an international electronics company with an annual turnover probably only marginally less than the entire budget of one of the smaller European countries.

She attributed her own rosy looks and obvious good health to her habit of swimming every day and took me on deck later to point out the beach she had swum to that morning. As I stared across the melting water I recognised it at once as the same beach from which I had swum a year earlier and could even make out the channels of sand I had negotiated into the green sea.

It would be nice to record that the rude good health of many islanders was due to their frequent immersion in the foaming waters around them but it isn't true. Certainly the people in our village are creatures of the seasons and, if they go down to a beach at all, it is only with their children for a few hours during high summer. As far as I can make out, even this ritual has a largely practical purpose, since it is clearly important that kids who live on an island learn how to swim.

(The last time Marylle and I ate with Nico and his family we were invited to look at an album of photographs, one of which showed Yannis as a boy about ten standing proudly at the edge of the sea. He had the thin face and big ears of many boys of that age and I was reminded of an almost identical photograph of me on the sands at Ramsgate which my mother persists in showing anyone in my company).

Since animals have to be looked after every day of the week, and healthy crops do not grow without care and attention, these swimming lessons are normally conducted by the women of the family. This means that the sandy beaches near Chora are deserted most of the year but in August are full of howling infants who have just been dunked in the sea for the first time. There will be other women in the water trying to persuade children to kick their legs as they tow them through the waves, and older ladies standing up to their waists wearing shapeless black swimsuits and enormous hats on their heads. I am told they do this because they have been informed that it is good for them to be in the water, even if they do not feel that it is advisable to move their limbs once in a while to take full advantage of it.

(There is something in the huge ease with which these elderly women inhabit their bodies that seems to be true of many Mediterranean grannies. I suppose most of them are from peasant backgrounds and have reached a position in their communities which gives them this obvious physical complacency. I have seen venerable old ladies in Spain march into the sea and stand there splashing water up between their thighs without the slightest trace of embarrassment and then return to the hot beach to take charge of their grandchildren again).

Of course there are a few souls on the island other than Marylle and myself who swim as much of the year as possible for reasons of both health and pleasure. This means in our case that we start entering the water in May and climb out towards the end of October, although it has been known for the sea to remain hospitable to mortal flesh until much later in some freak years.

The swimmer I remember with great admiration for his stubborn persistence was an old man who must have been in his late eighties. He was a frail stick compared to some sturdier specimens on the island and was always accompanied by another senior citizen who turned out to be his son. Whenever we went down for an early swim during the summer months we would usually see them together about fifty yards out in the water making for a line of rocks jutting out into the sea. The son always swam in stately circles near his father, who was easy to miss at first, since he used such a hesitant laborious back stroke that he seemed to be submerged most of the time. It was only after looking around carefully in the area where the son was swimming that we would finally notice two emaciated arms emerge from the water with agonising slowness before disappearing again.

There are a number of handsome beaches on Andros and Marylle and I try to go as often as possible to a couple which are often deserted in summer, since they can only be reached down several miles of long twisting dirt tracks. These are best negotiated in old cars by people with rubber spines but the beaches at the end of them are startling in their almost savage beauty.

The first time we visited the wilder of these two beaches we were with Yorgo, the owner of the inimitable café bar at Vourkoti, who had invited us to look at a small part of the great tract of land he owned and, incidentally, to pick some of his marvellous grapes. Since he wanted to impress us with the sheer scale of his domain, we had parked the car up in the mountains and then descended down rocky paths that made walking difficult even for goats.

The grapes were clustered low on ground watered by natural springs and, after admiring the trough he had made in which they were trod, we called in at a rough little house to drink water from a jar with a flat stone for a lid. It turned out that the house belonged to Yorgo's son, who was a priest in Chora, and that he used it when he was working on the land he had in the area. There was a crucifix above a plain iron bed in one room and a faded blue priest's robe hanging in a high niche in the wall that obviously served as his wardrobe.

We had to cross shallow water and then through some oleander bushes to get to the beach and Yorgo told us to go on ahead when we came to them. The beach itself was composed of a million polished white stones the size and shape of cricket balls and sloped down sharply beneath stinging waves into a cavernous green sea. We undressed quickly behind a deserted rowing boat and were rolling around in the water when Yorgo appeared from out of the coloured bushes wearing huge billowing black trunks down to his knees.

I don't think I had realised until that moment quite how big he was and, although the temptation was to be amused at someone his size clad in what looked like vast rugby shorts, my first thought was that he might be too heavy for such a splintered glassy sea. This was absurd of course and, after crossing himself solemnly, he walked into the water up to his chest and began swimming with the easy grace of one of the larger mammals.

Afterwards we rested in the shade of one of the oleander

bushes and ate some of his sweet grapes while he told us that he used to swim there quite often in the days when he roamed the area with his sheep.

— It's probably the best beach on the island, he said, but be careful if you come back by yourselves and decide to swim down that end.

I glanced down towards where the glittering white beach curved away from a group of dilapidated farm buildings.

— What's the problem then?

— There's the iron wreck of a boat in the water. It can be dangerous if you don't know it's there.

— What kind of boat?

— They say it's a British Army landing craft. I suppose they tried to land some men here during the war.

When we have small children with us Marylle will use another beach not far from Chora itself where a stream empties itself into the sand near some rowing boats only a few yards from the edge of the sea. There is a colony of ducks waddling about on its banks most summers, although I am told that most of their tiny chicks usually fall prey to large birds, but I never fail to be astonished by how green and placid the scenery is on either side of the wide stream.

I have strolled up its banks on many occasions and each time it is like walking back into my green boyhood in the Weald of Kent. It is true there isn't a buttercup in sight, and there are patches of canes growing between plane trees, but little blue swallows and dragon flies make a carnival in the air and, if I move with too thoughtless a tread, startled frogs leap from my path into the shallows.

Sometimes it is only the sight of the occasional lemon tree behind pastures where cows are grazing that makes me remember I am on a Greek island and not in the land of bluebells and hop gardens. The smell of frying squid from the taverna near the beach, not to mention the bouzouki music from its loudspeakers, makes it abundantly clear where I am as well, and then I breathe in the giddy sunlight and start to feel almost Greek again.

There are a number of streams on Andros and they all owe their existence to a combination of rainfall and the water which is reputed to run under the sea to the island. Although I didn't know it at the time, the stream running through the church in our village, which Papa Andreas had blessed while we were watching the stormy ceremony at Chora, was alleged to be the most sacred of all at one time.

The story goes that it had been the site of the famous temple of Dionysos, where water ran as pure wine once every year in ancient times, but James Bent didn't believe it and neither do I. He didn't because there are no other traces of antiquity in that part of the island, and I don't because I just can't associate the frenzied god of wine with the hard-working farmers living around our valley.

The only one who strikes me as having the looks and spirit of a modern Dionysos, as well as, incidentally, his own very lively wine, is Nico, and he is a family man who has little time left over from farming his property for too many drunken revels.

CHAPTER TEN

*I*T WAS JUST A WEEK BEFORE EASTER WHEN WE returned from London but I had a couple of appointments in Athens before we could catch the ferry to Andros. I was dying to see the house with all the rustle and surge of spring around it in the valley, although I knew that Antonis would have waited until we got back before he did much more work on it. There was no doubt about the season, even in the Athenian suburbs, and there was a riot of new greenery everywhere, with only the occasional poppy and patch of white marguerites proclaiming their different colours.

There was also no doubt about the approaching religious festival and solemn church music seemed to be on every car radio we heard instead of the usual bouzouki sounds. The whole of Greece commemorates Easter with a mixture of devotion and fervency which is peculiar to itself. It always seems to me that there is a terrible fascination with the pain of the crucifixion in Spain, for instance, and I am made uneasily aware again of the fatalism and cruelty which lay at the heart of that culture once. There is only a vast sadness about the crucified saviour in Greece, however, which manifests itself mostly in a kind of apathetic fasting, but what everyone is really waiting for is the great explosion of joy that comes with the extraordinary announcement that Christ is risen.

It is always more clear to me in Greece than elsewhere that this huge sense of nervous expectancy is intimately bound up with the renewal of green life in the earth. It is also difficult not to get the additional feeling that, because of its own history, the country as a whole identifies itself in some profound way with Christ's suffering and dreams urgently of his release from pain. While true believers in Spain will sometimes flog themselves with barbed whips until they bleed, the Greeks simply dye boiled eggs a vivid red to symbolise divine blood and then use them to celebrate Easter Sunday.

Of course all this has become commercial to some extent and there were shops selling these scarlet eggs a couple of days before we sailed to Andros. Other shops had closed down, as I discovered when I went for a haircut, and a number of Greeks had already killed themselves on the roads setting out early for the towns and villages they had left to seek their fortunes in Athens.

The air was thick with greetings as people wished each other good luck but the only person who made a point of saying that she hoped it would be a peaceful time as well was an elderly Jewish lady I knew. We had become friendly shortly after I arrived in Greece and I had slowly learned that she had come from Salonika, where most members of her family had been among the forty six thousand Jews from the city who had been deported to Auschwitz during the Second World War.

When she discovered that I had once lived in Spain, I also learned that she was a descendant of those Jews who had been expelled from Spain in the fifteenth century and been allowed to settle in Greece by the Ottoman Turks. She even spoke a very formal Spanish, which she had learned from her parents, although I understand that the language of her community in Salonika had still been essentially the same as that which they had spoken in Cordoba and Seville five hundred years earlier, even though written with Hebrew characters.

I used to meet her at a coffee house outside Athens, where she was normally surrounded by a host of chattering Greek ladies, none of whom knew her extraordinary history. She was a remarkably balanced lady considering the horrors that had attended her life, although it is true that she smoked a hell of a lot and had a voice like a rusty angel.

Marylle and I finally caught the ferry to Andros on the Thursday morning and ran into Antonis as soon as we went down to the house. As a matter of fact, he had heard us coming down the steps and had the door open when we turned the corner so that we wouldn't ruin his handiwork. It turned out that he had worked ten days for us while we had been away, including the repair and painting of two ornate old doors that Marylle had wanted to keep.

He had also planted four small hydrangea bushes on the wall outside the house next to the communal channel of water and, as we saw to our delight when we went down to inspect the garden, plots of peas and onions near where the broad beans had started sprouting. Although he seemed as bright and meticulous as ever, I had the feeling that he was worried about something as he stared at me with one glazed eye, but I didn't ask him about it at the time.

There was a bitter crackling of small fireworks all over the island the next day as the kids geared up for midnight on Holy Saturday when they are allowed to startle the night with bangers and rockets. The theory is that they celebrate Christ's resurrection in this way but, in practice, they start tossing the things about long before the priest has made the great announcement. I haven't spoken to a single Greek who doesn't deplore this habit, or not agree that it can be dangerous for people coming to church late in the dark, but, since it is almost a crime in Greece to chastise children, nothing is ever done about it.

When we went to mass at the village church that morning Papa Andreas had a full congregation, with some younger children having climbed up to the gallery and, even, into his high pulpit. There was a beautiful sprawling mass of scented stocks and roses on top of Christ's bier, inside which was an icon of the wounded saviour, together with a copy of the Gospel. I could hardly understand a word of the service but the prevailing atmosphere of sadness and compassion was so affecting that it was impossible not to be moved. At that moment I could well believe the stories I had heard about some people who drink only water and vinegar mixed with spiders' webs on Good Friday in order to experience something of Christ's physical distress themselves.

Later in the evening we drove down to Chora and stood on the steps of the town's main church as the service came to an end and the priest emerged behind a man carrying a tall heavy crucifix. Just before the sacred bier was carried out on the shoulders of four men there was a wild shrieking as the town simpleton ran from the church and stood there in his saffron robes swinging an incense burner with furious energy and determination.

Although some of the smaller children taunt him, he is treated with affection by most of the townspeople and is always given an important role on these occasions, which clearly help bind him to the community. I wasn't surprised that his role had changed this year, however, because he had nearly caused a serious accident the previous Easter, when the weather had been quite different. He looks to me as though he suffered brain damage at birth and, apart from making a high whining noise a lot of the time, has a tendency to panic when he doesn't understand exactly what he is supposed to do. On this occasion he had been given the high cross to carry but, when a strong wind had torn at his robes, had staggered about in alarm, with the crucifix, which was almost his size, scything around him dangerously.

After the church had emptied we went back down the steps to watch solemn processions of mourners from the other churches in the town following their biers. It was a cool dark night but there were rivers of moving candles everywhere as the different congregations shuffled along behind their priests.

The idea was for the processions to meet at the main square in the town, where there used to be a massive gate in an archway to protect against pirates. It was obviously going to be a squash there, however, so we decided to retreat to a bar for a late brandy.

There are three large orthodox churches in Chora but, while coming back from a walk to the ruined little Venetian castle at the end of the town the following morning, we saw directions to a Roman Catholic church painted on an arch in an alley. Marylle hadn't known it was there, even though she had been coming to the island for more than twenty five years, and we followed the signs to a tiny little church set back around the corner.

There was nobody inside but it was obviously kept in spotless condition by someone and there was a room to one side of it which had twelve empty chairs arranged around a long refectory table. The church was hardly big enough to contain more than fifty worshippers and the vaulted ceiling was a bright sky blue. The pictures around the walls were a strange mixture of those from the Roman Catholic and Greek Orthodox traditions.

I still haven't discovered who the twelve Roman Catholics are, but whoever looks after the church doesn't believe in wasting good earth. As we left, I noticed that the little garden inside its gates was crowded with crisp lettuces, spring onions and mint.

We spent the rest of the day pottering about the house, or out on the terrace watching the bird life in the valley, and were tempted to spend the last hour of Holy Saturday at the village church. An hour before midnight, however, we drove down to Papa Yanni's church in the next village, where we had arranged to meet Katherine, a jolly Mancunian redhead who teaches English in Chora, and Mary, who works in London but visits the island with her husband whenever she can.

The church was crowded and, as the people inside moved around, there was a harsh crackling from the bay leaves strewn across its floor, accompanied by the occasional brutal report of a firework being exploded somewhere. When the ceremony reached its climax Papa Yannis and his retinue moved outside the front door of the church for the last solemn moments. As he raised his arms at midnight to declare that Christ was truly risen the church bells immediately started competing with the mad clattering of the fireworks to rejoice at this momentous fact.

The custom after this is for people to make their way home, or to a convenient taverna, and celebrate the breaking of the period of fasting with a special soup and the bloody eggs. It was pointless trying to move anywhere while the kids were still tossing their dangerous toys around, however, and we waited fifteen minutes in the grounds of the church before making a break for it.

We started off our meal in the taverna with the traditional Easter soup made from chopped lambs' entrails, rice and a broth from egg and lemons flavoured with dill. If this sounds like something the three witches in Macbeth might have cooked up one stormy night, I can personally guarantee that it is really delicious and almost justifies the fasting that is supposed to precede it.

Afterwards we were given our Easter eggs and spent the next five minutes tapping them against each other. This is an important bit of theatre in the proceedings and the person whose egg doesn't break after the full round of tapping is thought to be in for a very lucky year. It was ironic that Mary's stout red egg emerged unscathed because her husband had just been told that he was very ill and she certainly wasn't expecting the sun to stay out all year for her.

We had eaten well but this ceremonial breaking of the fast in the early hours of Easter Sunday morning is only the beginning of an orgy of consumption for the rest of the day. It is essentially a communal filling of the belly with all the bright tastes and flavours of spring and a baby lamb or goat is always the sacrificial centre of the feasting.

Although the lamb is usually roasted slowly over a trench of coals in most of Greece, it is cooked in the oven in Andros, but Marylle and I were invited to a lunch party later that day by friends who live most of the year in Athens. This meant that the lamb was spit-roasted and that most of the other delicacies were done to a nice turn on a fancy barbecue.

It goes without saying that the new wine was also drunk in Falstaffian quantities before everyone began collapsing slowly towards their beds for the next few hours.

___

I was still in a bit of a stupor when I woke the following morning, and it wasn't until I heard the birds calling to each other in the trees and the waterfall plunging away at the corner of the path that I realised where I was. After a few moments I became aware of a distant frenzied shouting and slipped on my track suit bottom quickly as it grew closer until there was a chaos of screaming and curses outside the house.

When I opened the door a sheep turned to glare at me wildly from the top of the wall where the water channel runs before taking another bite out of one of the little hydrangea bushes that Antonis had planted for us. The wall is about six feet high at that point and, on the other side of the channel, another wall of stones rises about the same height to an orchard above it. I had meant to have this wall stripped of its ivy and wild blackberry bushes at some time but the sheep had obviously decided to do this itself.

This may have seemed a good idea to the animal but it clearly wasn't to its owner, an elderly man I hadn't seen before, who was capering up and down on the path and making all the noise I had heard. He looked up angrily when he saw me, as though I had built the wall there myself just to tempt his sheep, and started throwing stones at it. I have no idea what he expected to accomplish by this but the animal simply skipped farther along the wall until it was perched on the little stone bridge which is built across the path to our house. It is below this bridge, on the other side of the path, that the water from the canal tumbles so uproariously, but there is also a small channel across it designed to take water to our mill if we ever get it to work.

I was amazed at the agility of the animal, because the bridge is fifteen feet high at that point and extremely narrow, but the owner wasn't impressed at all and I thought for a moment he was going to attack me as he turned and shouted furiously. After a moment I realised that he wanted me to get hold of a stick or something so we could mount a two-pronged assault upon the beast. I grabbed a broom from inside the house and waved it threateningly at the sheep from below the bridge until it shuffled backwards in alarm before turning to pick its way back along the top of the wall. When it saw the man waiting some dim sense that it was in trouble made it try to reverse direction but I flourished the broom once more and it stepped back down reluctantly on to the path again.

The last memory I have of that little scene is of the angry owner holding the animal by its front legs with its dirty matted head between his legs as he dragged it away down the path.

I didn't catch what he screamed at me as he turned the corner but I decided that territorial rights were at stake here and shouted back at him.

— What about my bloody hydrangea then?

There seemed to be something a little awry about that particular day anyway, and I spent most of it being surprised by the singularity of the world around me. At the café bar later I sat trying to read a Greek magazine and looked up to see a young boy pushing along a single skateboard with one foot. This wasn't strange, of course, but there was also a handsome bird cage balanced on the skateboard with an apparently unflustered parrot inside enjoying its ride.

When I went back down the steps to the cottage there were a number of sheep munching away contentedly at the greenery on one of the terraces of land opposite. There are five cultivated terraces across the stream at that point which belong to a couple called Dimitris and Hariklia and they are probably the most tidy and presentable in the entire valley. A lone donkey on the terrace above the sheep gazed down enviously at them and something of the economic logic of that kind of farming began to dawn on me. It clearly made sense to use the sheep as slow lawnmowers which also provide manure until each level was more or less ready to be prepared for its new crops. At the same time, the animals were fattening themselves up by their ceaseless feeding and could be relied on to produce a profit from their wool or meat after they had helped bring the land back into good condition again.

This was all fairly logical but didn't explain the antics of several other sheep down on the next terrace who seemed to be challenging each other, like woolly kids in a playground, in a series of threatening manoeuvres which they never seemed to complete. They would back away from each other and then pretend to charge before almost perceptibly shrugging and start munching the vegetation again.

Shrugging my own shoulders, I walked on down the steps until I came to a wild rosemary bush which tumbles down from a wall below Papa Philippos's garden. It was covered with a beautiful froth of pale lilac flowers and was alive with thousands of bees making a noise like massed violins on heat.

As I stared at the bush almost mesmerised by them I saw a little flash of bright colour from the corner of my eye and turned my head to see a lizard on another wall. It had a wisp of something that looked bloody in its mouth but on closer inspection turned out to be a tiny scrap from a poppy petal. It was clearly puzzled by this strange red insect it had found in its jaws and was shaking it from side to side like a dragon with a discarded cape.

After a while it became aware of me, however, and dropped the offending item while it crouched there on the stones with a pulse quivering nervously down the length of its throat. I had time to see that it had five delicate long toes on each foot before I started to feel guilty at giving it such a fright and deliberately made a movement. It scuttled at once further down the top of the wall and paused at one point to feel its way by brushing the surface with its two front feet before disappearing into a crevice.

I was beginning to realise now that this lunatic activity around me was probably because of the season itself and that all the new life was giddy with a huge nervous excitement. Back at the house I sat on the terrace for at least a couple of hours trying to become conscious of everything happening in the valley. The most obvious change was in the sheer mass and persistence of the vegetation around me, with the stone walls seeming to foam with ivy, and the trees brimming with leaves. It had also rained quite a lot earlier in the year and the stream was rushing down past the garden as though it had just been released from some dark underground prison into the sunlight. The whole impression was of a tremendous renewal of chaotic dancing life and it wasn't difficult at all to imagine water nymphs whirling above wet boulders in celebration of some extraordinary event.

There was something bothering me, however, and it was only just before I went back into the house that it suddenly occurred to me there had only been one hawk circling above the valley during my reverie. The female partner had to be on her nest somewhere and I wondered how long it would be before the young birds were being taught how to stoop in the air and drop for their prey.

A couple of days later Marylle went back to Athens on her own to sort out something to do with the music festival on the island she had been involved in trying to organise. As far as I could understand there was some problem in trying to raise the money for it and she was hoping to get in touch with Bambi Ballard, who seemed to have developed spring fever of her own and couldn't be found.

I spent most of the time while she was away making a small flower garden on a patch of land below the terrace and clearing stones from the earth outside the millhouse where I intended to grow herbs. There wasn't a lot more to do on the house itself now, but we needed new beams in one of the rooms on the bottom level and Yorgo had agreed to do these when he came in August to lay flagstones on the terrace and build a small patio down on the lower level.

When I wasn't playing at being a gardener I would sit up on the terrace again and watch birds I had never seen before revelling in their intricate aerial games. There was a period of about a week when the valley was full of flashy little strangers who made me breathless just watching them perform the fastest ballet in creation. I was particularly entranced by a flock of beautiful wide-bodied gold and black creatures who appeared out of nowhere one day and proceeded to whirl around the trees in marvellous formations like little flying drum majorettes.

I managed to drag Antonis out to see them but he just shrugged and said he had no idea what kind of birds they were. They were quite distinct in their appearance though and, after having looked through the pictures in several ornithological books, I think they must have been golden orioles.

Antonis was turning up to put the finishing touches to the large room with the huge fireplace only when he felt he had enough energy for the work now. It didn't matter to me when he came, because he had his own key anyway, but I didn't like seeing him so depressed. I knew he was upset about his sister, who had been diagnosed as having a serious illness a couple of months earlier, but he was also still having problems with his eye and told me one day that he could hardly see out of it at all.

I stared at him.

— You ought to go and see an ophthalmologist.

— There's one in Chora I went to last week. I told him I got some asbestos in my eye but he said I had cataracts.

— In both eyes?

— That's what he said.

— Well, at least they can be operated on these days without too many problems.

He hunched his shoulders and looked down at his elegant hands.

— I haven't got the time to have an operation. There's too many other things that have to be done.

It was coming up to the end of April now but spring wasn't over and the valley was still alive with surprises for me. I was raking the ground outside the millhouse for my herb patch a couple of days later when a hedgehog came shambling down the path towards me. It couldn't have been more than nine inches long and I assumed I had disturbed the area where it had been sleeping. There was an aggrieved look about it at any event, like a disgruntled spectator who had been asked to move at a cricket match, and I could have sworn it looked up at me indignantly as it waddled past my feet.

Antonis was showing me how to run the water from the communal channel into the garden the following afternoon when I noticed what I assumed was the same hedgehog dozing near the broad beans. I didn't want it to drown and it was Antonis who finally lifted it on to his spade and tossed it into a bush over the other side of the path.

When I spoke to Marylle on the telephone that evening she

said that it didn't look as though the music festival would get off the ground that year. Apparently the shipowner who had offered to help finance it was preoccupied with some problem in his family and Bambi had promptly switched her energy into trying to help the cause of American Red Indians. I shouldn't be at all surprised to see her appear on the island one day wearing a feathered headdress and escorted by a couple of muscular chieftains.

Walking up to the café bar afterwards I stopped to look at one of the most amazing displays of animal behaviour I have ever seen. There were only five ewes and three lambs on the terrace opposite now but scarcely any greenery on it left to eat. I was watching one large ewe and a smaller one trying to get some nourishment from the branch of a tree on the ground when they suddenly backed away and launched themselves at each other.

It was the first time I had seen ewes butt each other for real and my first thought was that the smaller one was going to get badly hurt. It didn't appear to be damaged by the shuddering collision of heads though and, in fact, started the next attack itself. The two animals carried on charging each other with an audible crack each time their skulls met until the smaller one turned aside and the other just butted it quite gently in its side.

The lambs had carried on foraging as this extraordinary duel had happened in front of them but now two of them also squared up to each other and pretended to attack. But as it was only in imitation of their elders, they soon lost interest and went back to searching the ground for more food.

Nico's son Yanni was in the café bar and laughed when I told him about the sheep who were almost as ferocious towards each other as rams.

— That's because there wasn't enough greenery for them, he said. Sheep quite often go crazy at this time of the year anyway.

CHAPTER ELEVEN

*T*HE BRIDGE WHICH CARRIED WATER FROM THE COM-
munal canal to our mill when it was in use until just after the
last war is outside my study window. I had vaguely noticed
some rather delicate little fronds growing out of it a couple of
days earlier but hadn't paid much notice with all the other
greenery bursting around. It was only when I got annoyed
with the emphatic moaning of a large bee outside my window
one morning that I looked up to see massed pink flowers on
the supporting wall of the bridge.

There were hundreds of them hanging from thin erect stems
and each one looked like two little plump lips arranged in a
ridiculously cute pout. I had probably taken a little too much
wine the evening before but I was taken aback for a moment
by this great spray of hanging mouths wearing the same banal
shade of lipstick. There was something almost provocative
about the way each pair of lips was pressed together and, as I
stared disbelievingly, the same fat bee settled on one flower
and rubbed its head demandingly against the soft pink mouth.

The luscious lips opened without protest and the bee manoeuvred itself inside them in a manner which might have shocked me had I led a more innocent life.

As I watched it wriggle out and fly away again Marylle came into the study and put her arms around my willing neck.

— Beautiful aren't they? You know what flowers they are of course?

— Remind me.

— They're wild snapdragons. Around here they call them Mayflowers because this is the month they always appear.

She was smiling and it suddenly dawned on me that it was the first day of May, which is when Greeks always hang up garlands of flowers and plants on the front door of their houses to embrace the new season.

When we went out for a drive later it seemed to me that the huge variety of new flowers on display had followed the visiting birds I had seen like the next act in a marvellous cabaret. There had been poppies and roses around earlier, of course, but, suddenly, as though a magician had stalked the island during the night, there was bright yellow broom everywhere. The sides of the roads were crowded with those kinds of mallows with small lilac-blue flowers and the fields were alive with blue lupins and many other flowers whose names I didn't know.

I had forgotten until we got back to the café bar in the village that it was Labour Day in Greece and a national holiday for those who didn't have farms to look after. This was why the café was full of people I hadn't seen before and the appetising smell of roasted goat came from its kitchen. The Greeks have a passion for driving into the country on days when work can be forgotten and our village is pleasantly rural without being too isolated.

There was also no doubt that Yanni and Antonis, the two friends who had taken over the café bar after Dimitri had gone back to Athens, had performed wonders with the place, even though they both had other jobs during the day. They employ a local boy to run it until they arrive in the evening and manage to attract not only the villagers, but also a floating clientele of young men on motor scooters from other villages in the area.

This might seem a strange combination of customers, but the villagers get comfortable seats on which to enjoy their snacks, and the kids have their rock music later in the evening, so everyone is happy. There is also the fact that the cooking is usually done by Yanni's mother, a woman of broad smile and ample construction, who produces the best moussaka I have eaten on the island.

When I asked her why goat was on the menu she said that it was a custom on Andros to eat it every May Day. It used to puzzle me why the Greeks celebrate Easter Sunday by eating thousands of lambs until I realised that they were sacrificial, and I suppose the same is true for the goats.

I seem to remember reading somewhere that Greece could double its forested land within a decade if people got rid of their goats but I can't see Nico doing that. He turned up down at the house shortly after we got back with two large sacks of goat droppings I had ordered to make the soil of our garden even richer over the next few months.

He had supplied me with one sack the previous year, which I had used where Antonis had planted the broad beans and peas, and I was so impressed with the riot of vegetation which had sprung up that I was now convinced it was the secret of a healthy garden.

I had seen goats on Nico's various bits of land before but there seemed far too much rich dark manure in the sacks to have come from these alone. When I asked him where he had got the droppings he looked at me in surprise and said he collected them up in the mountains where his wild goats spent their lives.

This was the first time I had heard about these goats

although, when I thought about it, I suppose a people with pastoral origins find it natural to let animals graze wild in this way.

— How many goats are there up in the mountains then?

Nico pushed his cap back on his head and scratched the side of his face.

— I don't know. About five hundred.

— How does each owner know which goats are his?

— We cut their ears in a special way when they are young so we know which ones are ours.

I was still puzzled when I looked down at the bulging sacks of droppings outside the mill.

— There's still an awful lot of dung here. It can't have been easy collecting it all.

There was a dark frown on his face as he stared at me but then it cleared as he slapped his knee and laughed until I thought he would choke.

— The only thing I need is a bloody shovel. It's all there waiting for me.

— I don't get it.

— There are lots of old ruined buildings up there on the mountains and the goats use them for shelter when it gets cold. All I have to do is go in and shovel the droppings into sacks.

— Do you go up there often?

He nodded.

— I like watching the goats. They get to know who owns them even though they're up there by themselves most of the time.

(These wild goats roam the mountain tops eating whatever scraps of greenery they can find. The more domesticated goats are hobbled so that they can't wander very far, although I am always astonished at how agile and adventurous they can be, even with a rope tied between their legs).

After Nico had left I dug part of the garden down on the second level and covered it with droppings before watering it as thoroughly as possible. A couple of days later his son Yianni came to help me plant some tomato and courgette seedlings I had bought at a shop in Chora. The following week he turned up with some cucumber seeds which we planted just as the first pods of broad beans were beginning to appear on the stalks of the rioting vegetables up on the level above us.

Although I grew up in the countryside, it was my first real experience of gardening and I was nervous of making too many obvious mistakes in front of local people. I tried to disguise my ignorance by saying that planting times were quite different where I came from but everyone seemed quite willing to help anyway. Their advice didn't stop me making a fool of myself but, fortunately, my disasters happened in private and I was spared incredulous laughter.

There was one occasion when I decided to use the water from the communal channel to irrigate the garden myself and, had I been able to arrange a video recording of the farce that ensued, I could have probably sold it for a respectable sum as a comedy routine.

I had helped Yannis do the same job a couple of times before and there didn't seem to be any difficulties involved that were likely to confound someone of normal intelligence. The only problem was that the communal channel, which started below the church further up the valley, passed underground beneath the terrace of the house above us, and there was an obstruction somewhere along its length. This meant that the water tended to overflow into the basement and, in practice, it was diverted into the stream a little way above the house most of the time.

This was a nuisance until the channel could be cleaned out but there was still enough water coming through to irrigate our garden if it was allowed to flow down to us in the normal way. I couldn't see any problem in this so I walked up the path and removed the slimy old shirt and large stone which had been used to divert the water just above the little field where Nico grew corn for his animals.

When water courses ordinarily down the channel it passes below the little waterfall to where a trench takes it into our garden provided the flow is diverted as it turns the corner. It took me five minutes to make a little dam there with some mud and another huge stone and then I hurried into the garden to wait for the expected torrent of water.

After a couple of minutes only a slow muddy trickle came spilling down from the trench and I clambered up the steps to see what was wrong. I realised at once that the stone I had used wasn't wide enough to block the channel properly and that the mud had been carried away by the water flowing around it. Fortunately, I had left a pair of dirty trousers I didn't use very often hanging over a chair in the bedroom and ran into the house to get them.

It still wasn't that easy to construct a dam which worked and I finished up sticking mud and dead leaves into the trousers to give them some ballast. When I jammed this lot into the channel with the stone behind to hold everything in place it worked perfectly. I stood there proudly listening to the soft thudding of the water as it cascaded into the garden, but then it occurred to me that I hadn't opened up the ditch which would take it into the patch of broad beans.

After rushing down into the garden again I saw the water was pouring over the edge of the terrace by the rose bush and grabbed a spade to make another little dam. When I had done this I made a breach in the earth bank around the broad beans to let the water flood in there. I had never noticed Yanni wearing anything but his normal working shoes when watering the garden but I certainly should have put on Wellington boots because my plimsolls were covered with mud almost at once.

There was no time to worry about this since the broad bean patch was quickly full of water and I needed to divert it into the onion bed. The trouble was the only place I could walk without treading in it was on the bank of the little ditch around it, and every time I tried this it collapsed under my weight. It was in an attempt to avoid this that I stepped back a moment into what was now soft muddy soil and promptly sat down among the fragile onion spires.

The chattering of the birds sounded like hysterical laughter as I picked myself up but nobody was around and I brushed myself down as best I could. There were great puddles everywhere in the garden and I had to hurry back up the steps and arrange my sodden trousers so that the water flowed on down the channel and not into the garden.

After making myself a cup of coffee I wandered out on to the terrace to look down on my handiwork. There was a donkey somewhere up on one of the terraces opposite making a noise like a wounded trombone and the waterfall was clattering away merrily behind me. I hadn't heard that beautiful sound in weeks and, when it suddenly occurred to me why not, I tore back up the path and hastily stuffed the old shirt back across the channel so that the water would be diverted back into the stream again.

There was quite a lot of water in our neighbour's cellar by this time but they were away in Athens and I was hoping it would have gone down by the time they returned. I didn't think anything else could have possibly gone wrong but when I got back to the house I saw that I had left great muddy footprints everywhere. Marylle was out shopping and I had just finished swabbing the floor down with a hosepipe when she came through the door and looked at me in surprise.

— You've been busy, I see.

— I don't see why you're the one who has to clean up all the time, I said airily. Did you manage to get the muslin?

Nico had advised me to dust our grape vine down with sulphur to prevent the new fruit being attacked by insects and said that he always used a muslin bag to do this job himself.

— There wasn't any in the shop so I brought you these instead, Marylle said. They should do the trick just as well don't you think?

I looked doubtfully at what she had pulled out of her shopping bag.

— I suppose so.

I warned her on pain of death not to laugh at me but she was almost in hysterics as I stood on the edge of the roof fifteen minutes later. There have been times in my life when I looked silly but I felt really absurd swinging a pair of pale nylon tights with sulphur in the feet out over the vine while trying to see if anyone was watching.

There was so much life happening around us in the valley that it seemed only reasonable to acknowledge it by going to church more often than I ever had before. Of course it was only at the top of the steps, and I knew most of the villagers by name now, but it was still an adventure of a kind and there was always something going on there to surprise me.

I turned up late on the Sunday morning after my charade with the tights and walked in just as a woman and a boy about twelve years old were taking communion. There was a baby over her shoulder and, when she came back to stand near where I was, the boy made faces at the infant until it laughed. The woman popped something into its mouth every time this happened and I realised after a while she was feeding it crumbs of holy bread.

There seemed to be affection in the air but I wasn't at all sure of what was going on when I saw two small lizards on the path going back down to the house. They were sniffing at each other warily like dogs, and I assumed this meant they hadn't been introduced, but before I could find out whether they had decided to make friends they sensed me and shot away quickly in separate directions.

I think that day must have been the beginning of summer because it was very hot and I heard on the radio later that it was over thirty five degrees in Athens. There were a lot of lizards around sunning themselves in any event and quite a few seemed to have lost their tails. I thought this meant they had been trying to eat each other but was told by a friend they were also attacked by birds. He also said they had disposable tails anyway and could grow new ones again within a few weeks.

It was clearly a time for feasting and the blossoms on the orange tree near our kitchen door seem to have attracted every bee in the valley. I stood there watching them gorge themselves while having my morning coffee and noticed that there were a number of what I think were May bugs on the foaming white flowers as well.

There seemed to be no animosity between them but every so often a green-winged bug would fall out of the tree on to the balcony and lie on its back. When I was sure what was happening I called to Marylle to come and look as well.

— Can't you step on it or something? she said. The poor thing is in agony.

— No it isn't. You just watch.

After a few moments the bug began rocking itself and finally succeeded in turning back on to its right side again. It stood there uncertainly and then began wandering around the balcony as if badly dazed and shaken.

— I told you, said Marylle. It can't fly.

The bug was opening and folding back its wings again now like a fussy little man with an umbrella he wasn't certain was working properly. This happened at least ten times but then it suddenly took off without problems and flew straight back to the orange tree as Marylle turned to stare at me.

— It was drunk, I said to her. It's the only possible explanation.

— I don't believe it.

— I've watched several of them fall out of the tree and stagger around like that one, I said. They're stoned out of their tiny little green minds.

It was a time of gifts as well and one morning Nico's elder brother Leonidas came around with a basket of large spiky artichokes which I had admired in his garden. The leaves were hard and sharp as little spears and I had bleeding hands after removing the tough outer ones even though I wore garden gloves. I finished up with a large saucepan full of plump little artichoke bottoms, and cooked them under the suspicious gaze of Antonis, who had come to work on the bathroom door that day.

Although he had admitted to me a few days earlier that he couldn't see at all out of one eye now, Antonis still refused to see a specialist and just walked around hunched and miserable all the time. I knew he was also worried about his sister, whose illness didn't get any better, and I felt as sorry as hell for him. There are many Greeks who seem to think that going to a doctor is an admission of defeat but I'm certain that Antonis believed it would do nothing more than simply confirm what the fates had already decided on for him.

It is difficult to imagine Antonis capitulating easily to human pressures but what the gods had in store was a different matter entirely. There is a marvellous Greek expression to the effect that some people will drown in a spoonful of water but this can be more a comment about temperament than courage. Antonis was a kind of human lightning rod who was extremely sensitive to notions of fate and bowed his sad head accordingly. It is true that there had already been such a lot of tragedy and bad luck in his family that it would have been remarkable had he felt differently about things.

He was trying to assert himself through work again that particular day and invited me in his usual way to share his lunch when Leonidas had left. We were sitting at the battered old wooden table eating wild asparagus from the mountains and new broad beans simmered in olive oil with dill when Nico turned up with his son Yanni to dig trenches around the fruit trees in the garden.

I noticed Nico glance at the little feast on my plate but didn't think anything about the way he had scowled until an hour later. We were all working down in the garden when his youngest son Stephanos appeared on the balcony waving a lunch box that this mother had asked him to bring down. Nico went up to see what was in it and a couple of moments later Stephanos came out on the balcony again to say that his father wanted to talk to me about something.

When I went through into the kitchen Nico was sitting at the table and had filled a plate for me from his lunch box. I was already full but I didn't protest, since there was clearly some kind of culinary pride at stake, and tucked into a second meal of artichoke bottoms and a succulent dish of spinach and lettuce leaves in a thin pastry case.

A couple of days later Marylle and I entertained her sister and a friend, who were spending their Whitsun break on Andros, to dinner out on our terrace. The main course was a mixture of broad beans, new peas and Leonidas's artichokes, which we had cooked gently with spring onions and dill in spring water, olive oil and lemon juice. We were proud of the fact that the vegetables were fresh from our garden and were happy to serve it with some of Nico's earthy wine from his own grapes.

It was a still evening although the air was alive with brilliant royal blue dragonflies which slowly vanished into deep shadows at the bottom of the garden. The excited chattering of the birds also died away as evening settled around us and, finally, all we could hear was the urgent liquid rustling of the stream as it flowed between the trees.

Suddenly there came the sound of furious cursing from farther up the valley and we could see the thin spectral flickering of a torch in the darkness. I looked across at Marylle as I recognised Papa Philippos's voice but somebody else started bellowing as well and another mysterious noise like a baby crying floated across to us.

This bedlam of profanities and cries of distress carried on for about five minutes as we smiled nervously at each other across the dinner plates and then stopped as shockingly as it had begun.

The café bar was closed when we walked back up the path with our guests but the following morning I ran across Papa Philippos sitting morosely over a coffee there. When I asked what the ructions had been about the evening before he said that a baby goat had fallen into the stream where it was quite deep.

The animal had nearly drowned by the time he and Leonidas had been able to rescue it and they had both got soaking wet in the process.

— Whose goat was it?

He stared at me indignantly.

— Mine of course. It weighed over twenty kilos and is worth quite a lot of money.

CHAPTER TWELVE

I HADN'T LIVED CLOSE TO A HEALTHY GARDEN BEFORE and was constantly surprised at the changes taking place in it now that the sun was shining again most of the time. There had been a sunken air raid shelter in the garden of the house where I grew up, and an elderberry bush down at the bottom near the allotments, but hardly any vegetables at all. This meant I never really appreciated how magical a garden can be, with the various plants growing at speeds of their own, like a living tapestry that delights with new forms and colours as it takes shape beneath a blue sky.

The broad beans were finished now but the tomato and courgette plants on the lower level were erupting beautifully from the dark soil. I had always thought that tomato plants needed to be staked but Nico got his son Yanni to lay giant twigs of broom on the ground between them so that the new fruit wouldn't get wet when the area was irrigated with water. There were no tomatoes as yet, although a few tiny flowers were visible, but the courgette plants had begun sprouting leaves like green elephant's ears.

I also hadn't realised before that sweet oranges can bear fruit at different times of the year but, fortunately, the people who had planted the garden had known this well enough. The largest of our trees, down near the stream, was still hung with enough oranges to provide us with juice every day, although there were some which had been sucked dry by mice and were no more than dry husks.

(When Yorgo, the old mason, appeared a month later he insisted on wrapping a plastic sheet around the trunk to prevent the mice climbing it, but I didn't really like the idea. It didn't improve the appearance of the tree and, anyway, I felt the wretched creatures must have been really hungry to risk climbing out along those high crowded branches with all the night predators around.)

At the same time the tree to the side of our balcony had shed its blossoms and new baby oranges had started appearing between its leaves. They were smaller than green marbles at that stage, of course, but what fascinated me was that they all had tiny white collars which looked exactly like miniature versions of those ruffs Elizabethan courtiers used to wear around their necks. I found the spectacle quite disconcerting in a way, as though there were hundreds of little green heads hanging from the tree, and it needed an act of faith to believe they would turn into ripe oranges later in the year.

Marylle and I were delighted with all the abundance around us but the luxuriant growth of ivy on the garden walls was a different matter. I had thought of trying to cut it away myself but then got talking to Michaelis, the brother of the man who had sold us the house, on the other side of the stream one morning. He had land there on which he grew vegetables and a muscular young man I hadn't seen before was helping him weed it.

— This is Yorgo, Michaelis said. Do you have any work for him to do?

— What kind of work?

— Anything that needs doing. He's from Albania and needs the money.

There were many Albanians around at that time, some of whom had entered Greece illegally, and Marylle and I had made friends with one the previous summer. He had been employed as a waiter in a local hotel but turned out to have played the French horn professionally in Albania and we were trying to help him find work with a Greek orchestra. The young man across the stream looked truculent, but was clearly fit and strong, so I asked him to turn up the following morning and tackle the massed ivy on the walls for us.

He worked very hard as it happened, and even broke my garden shears as he hacked away furiously in the sun, but it was difficult to feel as sympathetic towards him as I should have done. I gathered that he had left a wife and young child behind in an attempt to raise money, and understood that he missed them, but couldn't help finding his resentment about the way other people lived a little alarming.

I don't know whether he sensed this but, after he had finished for the day and I had paid him, I discovered that he had left the ivy he had stripped from the walls lying on the path leading down to the stream. There was so much of it there that even the mules couldn't have got past without difficulty and it took me an hour with a stiff broom to sweep it into two great piles on the bridge.

A couple of days later Michaelis volunteered to help me burn it on a shallow bank at the edge of the stream and I found myself tramping through the water with forksful of ivy over my shoulder. Michaelis produced some oil and we soon had a blaze going which I fed with more ivy and other plant debris until flames roared away towards the sky.

I was terrified that they would catch the branches of a large plane tree near the bridge but Michaelis joined me in the water with a rake to push the burning ivy a little further upstream. After a while the fire slumped down on the bank and little twists of burning vegetation hissed as they fell into the water. I was so relieved we hadn't set fire to the whole valley that I started to dance without thinking where I was and finished up on my back in the water.

Michaelis looked at me without expression as I struggled to sit upright and pull strings of wet black ivy from my face.

— What are you going to plant now that your broad beans are finished?

I gaped at him.

— I hadn't thought about it.

— It's time to plant string beans now. I can let you have some if you wish.

— That's very kind of you.

He stared at me gravely when I got to my feet as though it was quite normal to see an Englishman climbing out of a stream at that time of day.

— I'll bring you some tomorrow. You'd better make sure the fire has died down in a couple of hours' time.

There were dragonflies skimming perilously above the stream when I went down later to look at the dying fire and it seemed to me that they were everywhere during the next couple of weeks. It was obviously their season in the valley and what struck me about them was not so much their extraordinary flimsiness as the tremendous sense of urgent and lustful play they all seemed to have.

Most of the time they were skittering around near water, of course, or attempting aerial coition almost every time they passed each other, but I also saw a delicate line of them on the supporting cable of a telephone pole a couple of times. I stood there one drowsy evening watching them change places with each other every few seconds and, unless they were engaged in some military drill for insects, were enjoying a game remarkably like musical chairs up there on the cable.

It was clear that hectic mating was going on everywhere and I take it that the behaviour of a swift I saw the following morning was explained by a cat prowling near her nest.

After driving down to the next village for milk I had parked the car when I saw the cat crouching in the middle of the road looking baffled and furious. As I sat there the swift came winging down towards it, only to swerve away at the last moment when the cat stood on its hind legs and flashed at it with a vicious and frustrated paw.

At first I thought it was something that had happened out of the blue, but then the bird, which had drifted back elegantly behind some cypress trees, suddenly came streaking back again and it was clear that it was playing a wickedly reckless game. I'm sure the cat had been expecting this new provocation, because it hadn't moved from its position in the road, but this time swiped at its tormentor with considerably less conviction.

This game went on for several more minutes before the cat finally slunk away like a bully from a strange playground and the swift soared triumphantly away into the blue sky.

There was nothing at all triumphant about poor Antonis's behaviour when he turned up at the house later that morning, however, and he slumped into a chair with haggard white face and hands between his knees. We hadn't seen him in more than a fortnight and he muttered something about having gone to Athens to visit his sister. It was only after Marylle had made him a coffee that he admitted he had also been to see an ophthalmologist at the same time.

— What did he have to say?

He was staring down at the stone floor and I barely heard his reply.

— He wants me to have an operation on my bad eye as soon as possible.

— Well, you'd better have it done then.

— I haven't got the kind of money he's talking about. He says the other eye has to be done next year as well.

— How much did he say the first operation would cost?

— About three hundred thousand drachmas.

When I looked across at Marylle she nodded her head.

— We can always lend you some if you want, I said. You can pay it back by doing some work for us when it's all over and you can see properly again.

When he straightened up there was a startled look on his face and he suddenly took his hands from between his knees and brushed at the sleek grey wings of his hair.

— I couldn't let you do that. The reason I came around was to collect what you owe me for the two days work I did last month.

I handed him the money and watched as he tucked the notes carefully into his shirt pocket before standing up.

— Why can't you let us lend you some?

There was a hunted look about him now and he rattled out something so fast that I didn't catch most of it and had to turn to Marylle when he had gone.

— What was that all about?

She moved her shoulders helplessly and I could see that she was feeling distressed.

— He said he would feel deep shame if he couldn't pay it back for some reason. There's a lot of pride in Antonis you know.

(The Greek word for 'shame' in this sense can also mean disgrace and has much the same reverberations as the word 'verguenza' in Spanish. They both exist on the other side of honour and are felt strongly by people who can be very touchy about their pride and dignity. There was no doubt that Antonis was very Greek in this way but, at the same time, he had the soul of an artist and this meant that his feelings were more important to him than anything else. I believe this was why he was prone to suffer more than most people, simply because his whole being vibrated when he sensed injustice or tragedy around him.)

I'm sure that even Nico wouldn't disagree with this and he used to say himself that Antonis had a delicate touch in his work which made him quite different to anyone else in the valley. Nico's own instincts were those of the fighter, of course, and I don't think he could allow himself to sympathise too much with a different sensibility in case his own spirit and energy were weakened in some way.

He was due to come around that evening with some eggs he had promised us but it was Yanni who arrived with them and said that his father wanted us to come to their house the following evening. There had been some talk before about going to see where they lived but we had no idea whether this meant we were invited to eat or not. Of course, we said we would be delighted and it was Yanni who turned up the next day to guide us up a long high path looking down over the valley.

Although there were houses perched above us, on the rim of the valley, the path itself was primitive and, when we passed a natural cave formed by huge grey boulders, I could imagine at once the adventures Yanni must have had as a child. There was even one point on the path where we could look down at our house and across to the great monastery high up on the mountainside opposite.

The house was smaller than I had imagined but Nico was waiting there like a lord of the manor to show us around his little estate. It was clear at once that every scrap of land was put to use and, in fact, there was nothing I saw that didn't contribute in some way to the household economy. There was a great wide spread of hooks suspended like a murderous coat hanger from beams at the side of the house, which was for hanging the pig after it had been slaughtered. Behind it was a long open pit with a grill over it where the various bits of the animal used for making sausages were prepared.

Although Nico had crops on different stretches of land all over the valley, he also had a domestic garden there which I gathered Yanni planted in his role as farmer's apprentice. It was in flourishing condition, of course, with great hairy courgette and cucumber leaves spreading everywhere.

After admiring this we walked to some outhouses where Nico's tough little black and white mongrel Bobby, whose main duty was to follow the mules everywhere, was waiting in his kennel. He was there to watch over three noisy and quarrelsome piglets, who squealed with rage inside their sty when they saw Nico, until he tipped some slops out for them. He watched them slurp down this greedily with a sly grin on his bright swarthy face and pushed his black cap back on his head as he turned to us.

— I have beautiful little pigs eh? he said happily. They grow big very quickly for me with all the good food I give them.

I didn't want to think about which pig would finish up on the hooks but I was beginning to understand the virtues that made Nico such a good farmer. The first was his earthy enjoyment of his own nourishing food and therefore his commitment to making his land as healthy and productive as possible. Since he fed his animals with crops from the same potent soil they were also in marvellous condition and no doubt fetched good prices when he had fattened them up enough for market.

The second was a more surprising virtue in such a rough and impulsive man and this was the way he organised his time with singular efficiency. I had gathered during the course of our various conversations that he owned, or rented from other villagers, about ninety 'stremmata' of land, which is a little over twenty acres. This may not sound a lot, but it was dispersed in lots all over the valley, and he had to commute between them on one or other of his mules.

At the same time he had over thirty animals, apart from his wild goats on the mountain, to feed at any one time. This didn't include the mules, as well as a donkey he had bought a few weeks earlier, which composed, in effect, a sturdy little haulage business in the valley for him, and were certainly not there to be sold for meat. The fodder for all these was stored in an old house he owned on land about three kilometres up past the next village.

The amount of work involved in making sure that this little kingdom operated smoothly, with every function harmonising to achieve the right pace and rhythm, was quite phenomenal to me. With so many animals, and no real pasturage, he had to grow a number of different crops for them and there was barley across the stream from us, for instance, and maize further up the valley. This meant there was always some land within his domain that needed to be tilled, planted or harvested at different times of the year.

Of course he had two sons, but the younger lad was apprenticed to a plasterer, and most of the time he had only Yanni to help him, although he was always up first himself for the animals. I was surprised at how hard Yanni worked every day almost without complaint for a young man with little social life, but then everyone followed Nico's lead and pulled their weight in the family enterprise.

The smell of cooking made it clear that we would be eating with them when we got back to the house but Nico was called away almost at once and his wife fed us little tasty dishes until he returned. She had just started barbecuing pork kebabs on a contraption which turned out to be half an old water tank when he strode in and said something that made them both roar with laughter. It appeared that a bed they had ordered for her parents a couple of months earlier had been delivered unexpectedly that evening and Nico had gone around to help install it in the old couple's bedroom.

As far as I could make out, the hilarity was about Nico having said to his mother-in-law that she should be careful in case the new bed started making her feel like an eager young bride again.

We finally went through into a spotless dining room where there was a huge open fireplace and an embroidered scene of wild horses galloping through water on the wall. The meal that came was marvellous, of course, but my eyes kept wandering to the embroidery, which Nico's wife told us had taken her six years to complete.

There was nothing remotely original about it but I knew from similar compositions my mother had carefully worked on over the years how much womanly anxiety and feeling had gone into it. My mother always said that she liked to make things with her hands that were homely and that was exactly what they were and why she did them.

⚓

It was dark when we left and Yanni lit the way for us with his torch until we came to the house opposite ours where Hariklia and Dimitris lived. Since they were usually up before dawn every morning, it was surprising to see lights still on but, when we went over to buy some eggs in the morning, Hariklia said that her daughter had been there on a visit.

Although it was only half past ten in the morning, she insisted on feeding us with some delicious greens steeped in olive oil. These turned out to be the new shoots of marrow plants, which she had apparently planted too close to each other and thinned out a couple of hours earlier. We mentioned to her that we were thinking of going out to look for capers that afternoon and she asked excitedly if she could come with us, so we picked her up a few hours later and set out in the car.

The first time I tasted capers was in France some thirty years ago, in a sharp vinaigrette sauce that was served with pig's trotters, and I fell for their dark green flavour. I never really asked myself then what exactly they were, but it was impossible not to be curious in Andros, since the pink and white flowers of the caper plant are everywhere in summer.

Nowadays I know that capers are the unopened buds of these flowers which have been soaked in salted water for three days and then pickled in seasoned vinegar after they are dry again. It always astonishes me how it was discovered that they could be made edible in this way, but then the history of food seems to be full of strange turnings which unexpectedly lead to pleasure.

The seeds of the caper plant tend to flourish in the arid soil of old walls and we had been told that the place to look was the stone paths of a village above Korthi. When we got there I parked the car near an old church and we walked through narrow streets that were completely empty. There must have been people living there, because we passed one crumbling house with five pairs of stained jeans drying on a rope in the garden, but we didn't see a soul.

There was an ancient olive tree with two trunks on the outskirts of the village and, below it, a small colony of dark ruined houses which had clearly been very handsome at one time. They were deserted now, but the stonework was beautiful and each had a slim chimney stack with four little rounded columns on its top supporting what looked like a stone witch's hat.

I find this side of the island quite sad in some ways since, despite the fact that it still has quite a lot of good land, many of the villages are in a state of neglect. This is presumably because most of the former inhabitants have moved abroad or, more likely, to Athens, although the evidence seems to be that it was quite busy and prosperous at one time. There was even a monastery near Korthi where, according to James Bent, many visitors came to worship once because miracles were alleged to happen there.

It isn't easy to imagine Hariklia pulling up roots and moving to a big city where she wouldn't have a garden to engage her. A small compact woman, who scurries around constantly doing things with her hands, we first met when it was suggested that her husband might be interested in watering the trees for us every week. He has a back problem from an injury at sea, however, and can only just cope with working his own land, so, in the event, we decided on Nico.

It was Hariklia who told me that the great bunch of garlic bulbs hanging in the boughs of an orange tree was there to protect against the evil eye and she was the first one to find the caper plants. She had skipped on down a rocky path ahead of Marylle and me and, as we followed her around a corner near

Hariklia with one of her chickens

a narrow field where a lone mule was tethered, we saw that the old stone walls were suddenly alive with flowering bushes.

There were thousands of tight little green buds on each one to be picked but those which had flowered already had attracted interested bees. This didn't seem to bother Hariklia, however, whose busy fingers were soon moving at incredible speed as she started to fill the large plastic bag she had brought with her. Since there were so many bushes around in that area, Marylle started on some on the other side, while I moved a little further down the path.

I picked my buds rather more slowly than Hariklia, not only because I was being very careful not to annoy the bees, but because their shape and texture fascinated me and I didn't want to damage them. The flowers were also quite beautiful, with each white cup full of fragile waving pink-tipped stamens, like something delicate and alive glimpsed under water, and a perfume which Marylle said later reminded her of magnolia blossoms.

When I straightened up at one point I saw that Hariklia had already stripped a couple of bushes and was now on the one next to mine. She was completely absorbed in what she was doing and it occurred to me that the women who gathered edible plants in neolithic times must have also had her fierce concentration and dexterity. I looked across fondly at Marylle at this thought and saw that she had angry tears in her eyes and was sucking at her bare arm.

— What's the matter?

— I've been stung by a bee.

— I was always told that if you dab some of your own urine on a bee sting the pain will go away.

— You would know something like that.

— Why don't you try it anyway if it's hurting a lot.

There was a slight flush on her face when she came back from behind the wall a few minutes later but I saw that the weal on her arm was not looking quite so angry now.

— Did it work?

She stared at me defiantly.

— I should have brought some lavender oil with me but it seems to have helped.

We had picked several kilos of capers between the three of us by the time the light started to fade but we still saw nobody as we walked back through the village. I had never seen Hariklia so pleased with herself and she chatted away to Marylle like an excited child as we drove through the violet evening. When she got out of the car she made us promise to come and eat with her the next day.

CHAPTER THIPTEEN

*W*HENEVER I EAT OUT WITH GREEK FRIENDS IN London they generally choose French or Italian restaurants with reasonably sophisticated food. It puzzled me at first why the same people always seem to prefer the most simple Greek tavernas when they are back in their own country. The only reason I could imagine was that they had an unconscious loyalty to the kind of food their ancestors had eaten and felt warm and secure in such traditional settings.

I still think there is some truth in this, but there was no way I could believe it was because of the quality of the food, which struck me at that time as awful. There always seemed to be boiled greens turning up on the table, possibly some slices of fried courgette or cold beans in oil, and, for the main course, either a tepid dish with minced meat or something cooked in the oven with macaroni.

It also took me a while to get used to the habit in tavernas of providing bread and cutlery and then just dumping various courses on the table for people to help themselves. This meant that everyone was dipping into the same dishes for part of the meal at least, which I thought was carrying familiarity a little too far. It's true that I didn't have the same objections to the wine, which was just as well, since I usually drank quite a lot to drown what I was eating.

I shudder now to think of how snooty I must have seemed to Marylle and her friends. After more than thirty years in London I had become so accustomed to eating out that I was in danger of thinking food was just something waiters brought to the table when I had chosen from the menu. I had forgotten that good food takes its life from the soil and is often prepared by the people who grow it.

There is no way of forgetting the human involvement with food in Greek tavernas, which can be such lively places to eat in I'm almost surprised people don't just pay to come along and listen. It was when I decided I was enjoying all the warmth and noise around me that I stopped thinking about the way meals are prepared in fancy restaurants and started to taste the food in front of me.

The first time this happened Marylle and I had gone out walking in a forest for three hours before sitting down at a country taverna. I can remember putting a forkful of greenery in my mouth and then savouring the pleasantly bitter taste mixed up with olive oil and lemon juice with a start of surprise. After this I tried a dish of boiled yellow lentils from Santorini, which had been mashed together and served with onions and more olive oil. It had a crunchy texture and an elusive nutty flavour that went well with the slightly sour white wine from the barrel we were drinking.

It was the first time I had started to feel enthusiastic about Greek food and I went on to devour some sliced beetroot with a garlic and potato sauce before the main course of plain roasted goat. Out of the taverna's window I could see the large garden from which a lot of the food must have come, and suddenly it dawned on me that what I was enjoying was the sheer earthy nourishment in the meal.

I had read the usual stuff about healthy eating before but don't think I had ever experienced the extraordinary pleasure of digesting simple food virtually straight from the ground. I was like someone who had spent most of his life listening to music on record and then been astonished to discover how different and thrilling a real live performance can be.

Of course not all Greek food is that wholesome, but a lot of it can be in country tavernas, and eating in them is always enjoyable. It sounds a little crazy but I really think I started to come alive again in that little forest taverna and remember that true pleasuré is always a matter of feeling connected back to the earth. When we left I could have embraced every living thing around me, and I can't say I have often felt that way after eating out in London.

I don't think I became completely addicted to the natural tastes of the earth, however, until Marylle and I had been living in the valley for a few months. We had become quite friendly with Hariklia and her husband by that time, and, one day, after buying some vegetables from them, Hariklia invited us to eat in their crowded little scullery downstairs.

As far as I remember, we had just a strange but pleasant salad, a mess of greens, and a couple of eggs each, which Hariklia cooked in oil over a bundle of flaming broom. It seemed to me that the very pitch and grain of the valley was in that little meal, however, with the dark slaty feel of its soil in the vegetables, and the taste of flint and stones in the egg yolks.

Of course, we had some of Dimitris's very robust wine at the same time, which may have made my judgement dance a little, but it was also true that I had never eaten a meal before in which every ingredient had come from the immediate locality. The moment I got this into my head I wanted to know exactly what edible plants there were on the island and something more about its traditional ways of cooking.

It may be because people are flattered to be asked, but nobody in the valley had ever refused to answer my questions, and Hariklia was no exception. Although she is a busy woman, she spent the next hour telling us some of her recipes and about the kind of weeds and vegetables she habitually uses.

It turned out that the fat little lobes she had mixed with spring onions for the salad were from a plant that grew wild in her garden and which I finally managed to translate as purslane. I remembered reading in some worthy book once that purslane had been cultivated for centuries in temperate climates, but I had never eaten it myself, although Nico told me later that it ran riot further up on the mountainside.

When Hariklia showed us what the plant looked like in the raw I realised that one had moved into our flower garden and decided to try it in a salad for ourselves that evening. Hariklia had used only the leaves, but we found that the tender parts of the stalks were edible as well, although the taste lacked a certain bite, even with the sliced onions straight from our garden.

After some experimenting we found that the salad came really alive when we added another wild plant to it, which we discovered later even Hariklia didn't know about. We had picked some of this the previous year after we had first eaten it in a salad made by the son of an old fisherman who had known Marylle as a young girl.

The plant grows on cliffs and other sites by the sea, and we had been told to blanch it in boiling water before pickling it in vinegar. I had a feeling then that it was probably rock samphire, but couldn't find a translation of the local Greek name for it anywhere.

When I was glancing through a book on salad plants[1] not long ago, however, I saw that the Latin name for rock sam-

---

1. «The Salad Garden» by Joy Larcom.

phire was close enough to the name we had been given to make it virtually certain. Again, I had never eaten the plant before in England, although I'm told it has become quite fashionable in recent years.

I don't doubt the entire valley is full of various wild plants and flowers that can be used in salads, but the only one I know that is cultivated by the villagers is Mediterranean rocket. After begging some seeds from Antonis, I carefully planted some in our herb garden, only to find a wild clump had sprouted quite happily by itself under one of our lemon trees.

It was also Antonis who pointed out to us where some watercress grows in the edges of a tiny stream not far from the bridge below our house. The stream meanders down from higher ground on the other side of the valley, and then into a little rocky basin near our neighbour's dovecote before spilling over it and down towards the bridge. We have to climb up some wet rocks to get to the plant but it is worth it, for it is a larger variety than I have eaten before, and has a sharp peppery taste that goes well in many salads.

The villagers may not experiment much with salad plants but, like most Greeks of a certain age, they know which wild plants and weeds are edible, and Hariklia, for instance, cooks them quite often. The generic word for all of them is 'horta', but the only one I knew they ate before I came to live here was the leaves of the dandelion plant.

Nowadays I have only to walk down the steps during summer months to get all the 'horta' I want. There are many edible weeds but the most common one in the valley, and certainly in our garden, is called 'vleeta', which has the unfortunate name of notchweed in English. It can grow several feet high, has a wealth of pointed leaves and tastes sweet and healthy when boiled and marinaded in virgin olive oil and lemon juice.

The edible weed, or wild plant, I prefer myself is called black mustard in English, I believe, and tastes best when it comes from the mountains, but I have also eaten boiled sowthistle and enjoyed it as well. I don't know whether the fact that the names for these plants are more musical in Greek reflects people's fondness for them, but as it happens there is not even a separate word for weed in the language.

I had never heard of them even in English before, much less considered making them part of my diet, but I assume that my great grandmother, who was from an Irish tinker's family, would have done. Unfortunately, I never knew her, although I hope she was something like Panayiota, a hunched and formidable lady of advanced years I fell in love with not long after I started living with Marylle.

It was Panayiota who first made me aware of the vast range of edible plants in the Greek countryside, although I never mastered any names at the time because I hardly understood a word she said. She was formidable to me, not just because of her dark and hungering character, but because of how she had sculpted herself against all the odds.

She was the oldest child in her family but, because her father had not wanted a girl, had been abused and made to leave school early. Despite this, she had taken classes later in life at evening school and learned how to bind books and make jewellery. She was the only person I ever knew whose employment was as companion to old people at the end of their lives, and she was looking after Marylle's mother when I first met her.

We became friends quickly and I looked forward to our trips into the countryside in search of the wild plants she clearly loved and understood. Wandering across fields, or along paths with green edges, she would swoop on some plant that didn't look at all edible to me with a harsh cry of delighted recognition.

Since she had elected to live with the dying, she had the respect of other people, and ran the kitchen like a benign witch when she felt the household needed feeding properly. The meal I most remember her cooking was a spinach pie, which is very popular in Greece, but this time prepared with various wild plants as well, including the leaves of common red-flowering poppies.

The only regret I had when eating this dish for the first time was that I didn't have a good wine at hand to do it justice.

I'm a slapdash cook myself and have put together a repertoire of motley dishes adapted to our taste from all over the Mediterranean. It intrigued Panayiota to see me at work in the kitchen, but she herself only cooked dishes she had known from her childhood, and got very nervous when I did anything different.

She was so scandalised at the way I was preparing a sauce one day she jumped up and down with excitement and I shouldn't have been surprised to see her fly up to a shelf and sit there screeching at me.

— You can't do that, she howled, or words to that effect in her highly idiomatic Greek. That's not the way to do it at all.

A couple of years after this we had another wild spinach pie, although this time also with notchweed and poppy leaves, cooked by Antonis's wife Mosca. Antonis was working for us pretty well every day at the time, and, since he always gave me some of his lunch to eat, I became slowly familiar with Mosca's talents in the kitchen.

One of the most popular meat dishes in Greece is meatballs, but there are many variations on the theme, and one day Antonis appeared with what he called 'hortokeftedes', or what I suppose could be termed 'weedballs'. They were absolutely delicious and I asked him if he could show me how they are made some time.

When he turned up the following morning he had with him a bagful of wild plants he had picked in the garden of his sister's house. It took me some minutes with the dictionary to work out they were mostly sorrel and white beet leaves, and that he had also brought along some tender spring onions from his own garden.

After making sure that we had the rest of the ingredients he needed, he washed and chopped the leaves and onions and mixed them with flour, eggs, cheese, olive oil, and seasonings. When the mixture was sufficiently sticky he carefully ladled large spoonsful of it into hot olive oil until each had grown an appetising brown crust.

It was still early in the morning, but it was impossible to resist both the smell and the appearance of those weedballs, so I made a quick salad, poured out some of Nico's wine, and we sat down with Antonis to a rare small meal.

I had learned quite a lot about how to eat well on the island since that first meal with Hariklia, but there was still a surprise for us when we ate with her after the caper hunt. She served us with another lively salad and then produced an omelette I had heard about before, but neither Marylle or I had eaten, which had onions and broad beans in it.

Andros' speciality is its omelettes, and there is one I'm still waiting to try made with the flesh of courgettes, but they are usually only available in private homes. There are a few tavernas which will cook them on demand, but the majority have standard Greek menus and open only in the summer months.

CHAPTER FOURTEEN

*T*HE FIRST TIME I REMEMBER GOING INTO A TAVERNA on the island with Marylle she finished up in tears. It was shortly before Easter and we had gone for a walk down to the harbour at Chora when a sudden fierce shower sent us running back along the seafront. We passed an open taverna owned by Leonidas, a friend of hers, which was usually closed at that time of year, and ducked inside with relief.

There was music playing from a radio somewhere, although the place seemed deserted until Leonidas and his wife appeared from the kitchen to stare at us in astonishment. It seemed they had opened the place up only to spring clean it before the tourist season started, but insisted that we stay there until the rain had stopped trying to destroy the pavement outside.

We sat drinking the brandies he brought us and I relaxed with the music moaning pleasantly around us until I saw that Marylle was crying.

— What's the matter?

She tried to laugh as she wiped a hand across her wet cheeks.

— The woman singing is called Marinella. She makes me feel so Greek that I can't help crying.

I wasn't sure I understood this, but since Leonidas was also a bit moist around the eyes as he looked sympathetically at her, and he is a former soldier with four strapping great sons, I decided not to say a word.

Seafront tavernas in Andros specialise in fish when they are open, of course, and only cafés and tavernas up in the hill villages usually have the traditional island dishes. This is because most of the people who run them have their own produce and animals and provide the kind of food they eat themselves. Since members of the family don't get menus, neither do their customers, and meals either depend on what is available that day, or have to be ordered by telephone in advance.

The most remote of these high places was Yorgo's café at Vourkoti but it was quite often full of young people who had driven up in a convoy of cars for a different and exciting evening out. It was an adventure to get there, and the meals were always marvellous, but there was never really enough variety to make it worth going there too many times. In any event, Yorgo decided to stop serving food not long after our visit with the marble workers of Tinos and now just concentrates on running his bar.

Marylle and I often go to another taverna up in the hills these days, which has the same kind of menu but is not so far away to drive. Although I enjoy the food, the main reasons I love eating there are its bustling family atmosphere and the spectacular view from its wide terrace.

The taverna is built on a high flank of the hill above our village and looks across the valley to a slumbering mountain on the other side with the lights of Chora below. The mountain slopes down to the sea behind the little town, but the distant horizon would appear higher than its lights if it could be seen in the darkness, and this can lead to some startling effects. We were sitting there with some friends one evening when we noticed that one glazed and staring moon was balanced delicately on top of another in the lower crescent of the sky.

We consoled ourselves with several flagons of draught wine while considering divine omens and freak atmospheric disturbances before it dawned on us what we were looking at. The invisible sea was spread far out behind the foothills of the mountain and it was simply that a full moon was reflected in it at the point where it seemed to rest precisely on the edge of the horizon.

We usually telephone before going to the taverna and it is always possible to order a simple roast chicken, or the famous potato and sausage omelette, but we have also eaten goat and other meat dishes there. Sometimes we don't bother with these, since we're both happy with the other dishes, which include round slices of young courgette fried in batter, a dip of aubergines and garlic, fritters made with the chopped yellow flowers of courgettes, grilled peppers, and salads. If possible, I try to eat there often in spring, since the young soft cheese will usually be from ewe's milk.

We just drop in if we happen to be in the area but this is always taking a chance on what might be happening on the evening. Sometimes there will only be a few customers, but these hill tavernas are also where local people celebrate baptisms and other important family events, and, occasionally, it will turn out to be bursting with noisy adults and excited children.

The taverna's owner also has an energetic brood of his own, who are usually busy chasing each other around the tables as people are eating, although sometimes the oldest girl will take orders from customers. A blonde child about ten years old, with the composure of a small princess, she is very strict about the whole business.

When she served us for the first time I earned her displeasure by ordering a plate of greens as well as a salad. As a rule one normally orders one or the other in Greece and she wasn't at all impressed by the fact that I wanted the two of them.

After clucking at me she moved on to take orders from other people at the table. Only when she was satisfied with what she had written down did she come back and stand in front of me again.

— Do you want salad or greens? I can't write down both.

It was difficult not to laugh at the stern expression on her face so I just shrugged and smiled apologetically.

— I didn't realise that. In that case I'll have a large salad.

She seemed to become quite fascinated by me for a while after this, but I had to take poor second place to someone we ate there with not long ago. He was a pleasant young man who a friend of Marylle had asked us to put up for a couple of days and nobody could have been more exotic to the children. It wasn't so much that he was black that fascinated them, as the fact that he wore his long hair in the Rastafarian style, and they had clearly never seen braided locks on a man before.

The little blonde waitress wasn't serving that evening but couldn't take her eyes from him as we sat at a table and finally came across to us. The young man laughed when Marylle translated the question she asked and bent his head so that she could touch his elegant black tresses with wondering fingers.

— Why do you wear your hair like that?

He looked enquiringly at Marylle and then laughed again.

— I like the way it looks. Don't you?

She nodded gravely.

— How often do you have to wash it?

— Twice a week. That's the only trouble. It takes a lot of looking after.

She was still digesting Marylle's translation of this when her tiny plump sister sidled up and whispered something to her. After frowning at whatever was said, the older girl looked up at him again.

— Can she touch your hair too? She's too scared to ask herself.

— As long as she doesn't pull it then.

I'm not sure that our guest had a moment free to enjoy his food that evening but the owner told us later that his children hadn't stopped talking about him for a couple of days afterwards.

We also eat at a couple of little tavernas when we go swimming at some coves on the other side of the island. The one we enjoy most has a good trade in summer and some appealing translations of its regular dishes for tourists. Marylle loves their fish soup with an egg and lemon sauce, I enjoy my glass of ouzo with a little plate of boiled octopus and roast potatoes, and we both consider their 'moussaka with home maid' to be very cheap at the price.

There is another taverna set in a green cup of land between hills at the back of this one which we certainly want to eat at some time. We stopped there for a drink recently and were told that it serves roast suckling pig and other delicacies on Saturday evening. It was full of families from other villages in the island on that occasion and the retsina was some of the most brilliant and shocking I have ever tasted.

The wine of Andros tends to be produced nowadays by small farmers like Nico, who always have vineyards and olive trees along with their animals and crops. It is kept in the barrel of course, and most of it is for their own use, although, fortunately for people like us, some does find its way into private houses and hill tavernas.

There is wine from the barrel available at some of the tavernas down by the sea, although most visitors usually buy bottled wines, but a lot of it seems to come from Crete. I find this a pity because a drive around Andros shows that there must have been enough vineyards around at one time to have kept everyone merry, without having to import from other islands.

It is even clear from talking to some of the older islanders that Andros wine was produced for sale to merchants in Athens at one time. This must have been destined for France, however, where a lot of wine from the Cyclades was dispatched after phylloxera had ravaged the vines there.

The Greeks have an appellation of origin system for their traditional wines but Andros isn't entitled to one. There is only one wine regularly bottled on the island and that is a superb blend from three different French grapes made by a shipowner with a vineyard there.

The only other bottled wines on the island I have heard about are the result of some wine still being left in a barrel at the time of the new vintage. In that case it is poured into old bottles of any shape or size with simple labels to identify the contents scribbled by someone in the family.

I live in hope of being invited somewhere and finding shelves of dusty bottles with grimy labels in some stone outhouse but so far it hasn't happened.

Andros itself was attacked by phylloxera in the early years of the century and, according to a lively and scholarly book on Greek wine[1] was substantially replanted by three varieties of black grape. I am sure this is true but, whenever I mention these to the farmers and hill people I know, they always throw back at me excitedly many other names I have never heard about before. Since Greek experts have apparently identified over sixty varieties in the Cycladic islands, however, I suppose this is not surprising.

There is a mild but touchy rivalry between the island villages about the comparative merits of everything they produce. I have only ever heard people grudgingly admit that the wine from another village might be drinkable, although the author of

---

1. «The Wines of Greece» by Miles Lambert-Gocs

the book mentioned above believes that the island's best red wines come from Korthi and Sineti.

Marylle and I have drunk several different wines from the hill village of Sineti and each was enjoyable in its own way. The only one that was a definite red in colour, and lively in character as well, was served to us at a dinner party. It certainly went well with the light food we were given, and was even refreshing to drink by itself.

As it happens, we had drunk another wine from Sineti at a taverna a few days earlier, and it could have come from a different planet as far as I was concerned. It had a rusty, rather than red, colour to it, but, again, it complemented the food we were eating that evening, which was mainly aubergines and roast kid, with its own earthy flavours. When I held some in my mouth there were overtones of minerals in it and something like the taste of a wet forest.

I have never drunk a wine that actually tasted of rocks and bushes, like the country priest's wine described by Peter Levi in his marvellous book[1] about his wanderings in Greece. This wine came pretty close to it, however, although I take it that the metaphor was really supposed to say something about the elemental character of most Greek wines at that time.

Most experts seem to agree that there is no point in comparing Greek wines, the majority of which are made from ancient grape varieties hardly known elsewhere, with wines from other European countries. There are a few Greek businessmen today producing wines based on French models, some of which are very successful, but it still seems a pity to me when there are so many interesting local wines that have never been bottled.

In a way I'm quite pleased that most wine made in Andros is only available from the barrel, because it's fun trying to find the wines we like from different villages every year. With

1. «The Hill of Kronos» by Peter Levi.

bottled wines the quality remains much the same most of the time, but new wine in barrels varies enormously every year depending on weather and other factors. This makes hunting a really interesting wine down after every new vintage something of an adventure and adds to the pleasure when we discover one to hum over.

The other reason we prefer wine from the barrel as a rule is that most of it in Andros is made without adding chemicals to the brew. There are, of course, a few people who do this, but I always know if we've drunk some of their wine at a taverna by the state of my head in the morning. The blessed pleasure in drinking a wine made only from grapes and time is that it leaves the head clear to remember it with affection.

Of course, some wine from the barrel will become thin and sour after a few months, but Nico assures me that this happens only when it isn't strong enough in the first place. Apparently, the way that wine is fortified naturally on the island is by boiling down some of the grape juice until it has reduced considerably and then adding it to the must fermenting in the barrel.

When I asked him how he knew the wine had started fermenting he laughed uproariously.

— It's like listening at a woman's belly for the new baby, he said. I just put my ear to the barrel and usually I can hear it bubbling within a couple of days.

We have become so fond of Nico's wine that we have made arrangements to buy one hundred litres of his must to make our own later in the year. I have been invited to join him and his sons tread grapes up on the mountain near where they grow. This is wine making at its most primitive, of course, and the must will have to be transported down from the mountain by mule in goat skins which have been sewn by men who have learned this special skill.

I knew that the skins were always from rams and when I spoke to Yanni, the merry sixty year old mason who works with Yorgo, he said the problem with female goat skins was that they leaked by nature. He was grinning at me at the time, however, and I take it that the real reason is because no female of any species is supposed to touch the grapes when the new vintage is being made.

The skins are sewn with the woolly outer hides turned inside and, although they are washed thoroughly in the sea before use, I have read reports that this makes some travellers feel sick after drinking the wine. This reaction seems to me more hysterical than anything else, however, and goat skins have been used widely to contain wine in Mediterranean countries for centuries.

I suppose they do contribute to the fairly strong taste of some island wines though, and it is true that Marylle and I have had some guests to dinner who couldn't stand Nico's pungent brew. On the other hand, we feel that nothing could go better with the kind of food we are used to eating in the valley now, and that both are rich with the dark flavours of its healthy soil.

Of course, this whole business of taste is very personal, and it can easily be influenced by many other subjective factors. We both still love to drink the prettier French wines occasionally, for example, but probably because I associate them with lifestyles in my past, they seem to have too much art in them for me nowadays. I leave the table feeling that I have been party to a civilised occasion but certainly not that I have come more alive.

I dare say that I respond to the more robust wines of the island because I feel that they are the natural beverage of men like Nico and Yorgo, the stubborn old mason. They are our friends now and have helped me find my way back to the centre of the earth again in a way they wouldn't understand if I tried to explain it to them.

When I lift my glass in the valley I feel in a way that I am saluting their ancestors as they pause from shaping their stone walls to sit in the shade with wine from the same deep barrel.

CHAPTER FIFTEEN

*I*N ANDROS SUMMER COMES WHEN THE VANS CONTAINing ice cream start arriving from the mainland and the cinema in Chora opens its doors. It is one of only three cinemas on the island, and is completely open to the sky. There is a large oleander bush to one side of it, which partially hides where the toilets are, and the screen is a huge curving stretch of concrete. The projection box is above a kiosk selling pop corn and the seats are made of some kind of reinforced plastic and bolted together in rows.

The first time I ever went to an open air cinema was in Florence after I had hitch-hiked there many years ago, and at the time I thought it was one of the most fascinating experiences of my life. The film was an American comedy featuring Humphrey Bogart and William Holden as two brothers in a romantic tangle over Audrey Hepburn. I couldn't get much more of a story out of it than that because the dialogue had been dubbed and I only spoke schoolboy French in those days.

What I recall vividly to this day, though, was the extraordinary spectacle of Humphrey Bogart, in black suit and Homberg, but still with his beautiful ruined mouth, speaking Italian out of one side with astonishing musicality.

Fortunately, films from abroad are not dubbed in Greece, and the subtitles usually seem masterpieces of compressed translation to me. After three years of watching films in Andros, I suspect I have picked up quite a lot of my Greek from these little captions, and can almost read them without moving my lips now.

It needs concentration, however, since the cinema seems to be full of children most of the time, who get bored easily if the action isn't fast enough, and enthusiastic if they like the film. I spent the early years of my working life on newspapers and the level of noise in the news room was nothing compared to the racket these kids can make sometimes.

Most people love summer, of course, but I always think that the Greeks have a special passion for it which shapes their lives in many ways. I dare say this has something to do with their history, and the sense that, for the time being at least, there is warmth and abundance for everyone, but it must also be because their country is at its most beautiful in sunlight. There is no doubt that summer in the Greek islands casts such a spell that it is sometimes difficult to imagine any other place where light could have first started flooding the earth and the seas.

At the same time such beauty can also colour the soul with a shadowy desolation and make people embrace each sunny moment a little too fiercely before it fades away again. It is a feeling which sounds like falling stars in Greek songs but can also lead to a melancholy fatalism in my experience.

I was talking to a middle-aged man in dry expensive swimming shorts last year who said that he saw no reason to stop smoking so much even if it was killing him.

— I have made my money and brought up the children, he said. Perhaps it is best to die while life is still so beautiful.

I swim less often than Marylle, who would have made an

appealing mermaid, but I can understand this sentiment in a way when I'm in the water looking back to land. There are afternoons when the view is only of rocks and churches melting together in the sunlight and everything looks so marvellously insubstantial that I'm almost frightened to climb out again.

I shouldn't think that Nico has ever felt this way, since he tells me that he has only glanced at the sea a few times since leaving his last ship, and scarcely ever leaves the valley.

We were expecting Yorgo and his gang of sprightly veterans in August but there was a lot of rubble to be cleared away first. I had agonised with Nico for a couple of weeks about where we should tip this until he volunteered the use of a spare bit of his land as a dump for the earth and stones.

He turned up with three mules strapped with metal panniers to carry it, together with his son, Yanni, and brother, Papa Philippos, with shovels over their shoulders to fill a patient wheelbarrow.

It took five days to remove the rubble and, in the process, the path outside our house and up past Antonis' sister's place to the dumping site, began to fill up, quite understandably, with mule dung.

I didn't say anything about this, although it was like walking through a narrow sewage farm every time I went up to the café bar, but, one day, Nico heard that Anna had been discharged from hospital and would be returning to the house within a week. He promptly borrowed our large stiff broom and set to work to sweep it all down the steps somewhere. I was rather hoping I could pinch some to put on my compost heap but he told me later that he had spread it all around his maize field.

— You should have told me you wanted some, he said. It can be very useful this time of year in several ways.

— What do you mean?

— The old people used to burn the dry dung outside their bedrooms.

— What on earth for?

— It keeps the mosquitoes away.

I'm always delighted with information like this, although, in fact, we had already provided ourselves with a chemical amulet against mosquitoes which had to be plugged into the electrical system to work. There are friends of mine who constantly mourn the fact that Mediterranean countries have mostly lost their primitive glamour, but, on the whole, we are quite happy with the way things are nowadays.

Personally, I always have liked to rough it a bit, but not all the time. When we travel we usually pitch tent under a tree somewhere one night and stay at a hotel with good food the next. In the same spirit we are trying to retain most of the original features of the house but also to make sure we don't live completely in the same primitive way. It is a question of establishing a rhythm between luxury and denial, adventure and responsibility, novelty and tradition, since this is the only way we know how to stay young for as long as possible.

If I lived in comfort all the time I would feel as though I was preparing myself for death, but I don't mourn for all the burdens and discomforts of the past either.

Nico's favourite mule, Psaroula, didn't look pleased at how uncomfortable she was when I found her with her head pulled up high into the branches of an old apple tree by her reins. She had been carting rubble away all day but it was early evening now and there were two thick sheaves of greenery tied on either side of her saddle.

I was trying to comfort her as Nico came back down the path and grinned when he saw what I was doing.

— I have to tie up her head like that or she'd turn it and start eating the horta, he said. She's as greedy as I am sometimes.

He spoke to her with rough affection as he loosened the reins before swinging his leg up and she shot off up the path faster than I had seen any mule move before.

The rubble was nearly cleared by now and I had been able to hear Nico keeping his mules in order as he shovelled stones into their panniers from my study window. I had become used to the strange rough exhortations he used with them but had only taken time to listen to them carefully these last couple of days.

It seemed to me that he had a vocabulary of about eight sounds and that the one he mostly used began with a kind of low warning roar that lifted gently into a higher more reassuring noise. There were a couple of short explosive roars which sounded much more ominous, and then some softer encouraging grunts.

I found it a little strange to see Papa Philippos working in a stained singlet and black baseball cap when I was more used to him in his clerical robes. It didn't occur to me at first that he wasn't asking for water all the time as he had before, but then he grabbed me by the arm one day with a huge grin on his bearded face.

— The doctor says my last test shows I have no sugar in the blood, he said. I did everything he said and now I'm better.

I looked at him dubiously, since I had seen him drinking a little wine, or ouzo, whenever he thought he could get away with it.

— What exactly did he tell you to do?

— He said that when I wake up in the morning I should drink the juice of a bitter orange together with some lemon juice and bitter almonds.

— Nothing more than that?

— Of course I also took the pills he gave me and drank much herbal tea.

A couple of days after the rubble had been cleared away Antonis appeared with his wife for the first time in weeks, so perhaps it was turning out to be a healing summer for him as well. I had heard that the operation on his eye had been a success, but that he was still feeling dispirited about his sister and wasn't eating very much.

Apparently, his sister was due to arrive shortly and they had come to pick up some of his tools while they were in the area cleaning her house. The first thing I noticed was that the slightly crooked smile with which he used to greet me was no longer there and that his face was more lined than I remembered it. He was also grey with what seemed to be a kind of moral fatigue but, on the whole, looked in better shape than I had expected.

We talked for a while in the kitchen after he had found what he wanted and I walked with them a little way up the path afterwards.

— It was good seeing you again Antonis. I hope you start feeling better soon.

He smiled wanly.

— I'm still in a state. I've never felt in such a bad way about things.

I noticed that his silver hair was still groomed beautifully as he opened the gate of his sister's house for his wife and suddenly thought of all the clever imaginative work he had done for us. In many ways he was a stranger in the valley because of his range of fine skills and fragile temperament. I knew people like him in London, of course, who also paid for being sensitive and talented with bouts of depression, but they were usually in rewarding jobs with kindred spirits around them.

It was a pity he was out of action for the time being, however, because he might have been able to help me with my mice problem. I hadn't been too annoyed about them eating some of our oranges but when they started on my ripe tomatoes I got really upset. Finally, and with considerable misgivings, I bought some poison, but there must have been whole tribes of them because it only managed to slow down the carnage of my beautiful red fruit a little.

I suppose all the creatures in the valley were engaged in teaching their children how to survive with so much to eat around. There had only been two hawks circling above the cypresses the previous year but now there were six who often flew very near each other. It was only when I realised this would have caused mayhem among rival birds did it occur to me I was probably watching parents giving their youngsters diving lessons.

Although I saw one or other of them stoop in the air to plunge downwards with folded wings a number of times, the dive was never completed and the bird would wheel away back up into the air at the last moment. It worried the pigeons however, and, when the family of hawks came near the dovecote, they would all take off in a great flutter of nervous wings.

There were also literally hundreds of baby lizards around on the walls or path every time I walked up to the café bar. Although some of them were no longer than a matchstick, they all came equipped with the necessary instincts, and would freeze into complete immobility if I got too near them, with their tiny heads tilted upwards to look at me, presumably because their nervous system had told them I was a large bird.

I came back from the café bar one hot morning to run across several sunning themselves on the path next to the communal water channel. As a rule they would come out of gaps in the stone wall on the other side of the path and scurry back in again if danger threatened. This time my shadow fell between them and the wall, however, and each one turned in panic at my approach and then sprang right across the channel of water into the vegetation of the bank on the other side.

It was prodigious leaping for any creature and I calculated that the equivalent for a human being would have been a standing jump across the Thames just below Windsor.

The tiny lizard which fascinated me was the one which had taken up residence in our house and I would see sometimes in my studio and at others in the bathroom. First of all, it was pink in colour, with rather elegant black loops around the lower part of its tail, and black-ringed pop eyes. Then, it seemed to be entirely on its own, unless there were others about the same size which took turns to come out into the open occasionally.

After a while we both grew fond of it, even though it was clearly terrified of us, and I took to calling it Freddy, after a boy in my childhood who could never be found once he had hidden himself somewhere.

As summer progressed there were occasional flappings of air in the trees, to remind us of the very strong winds that always come before August is over, but usually the weather was still and very hot. We would have our meals out on the terrace most evenings and feel the air cooling around us as we listened to the stream moving between the violet trees.

The north wind known as the Meltemi began blowing in earnest almost on the same day that the Fast of the Virgin Mary started. This isn't so widely observed as the fast for Lent, but there are church services every evening for the same period until August the fifteenth, which is the feast of the Virgin Mary.

It is also the period when enormous numbers of Greeks take their summer holidays, although it always strikes me as odd that they should choose the two weeks when the Meltemi is at its strongest. Of course, the wind can help lower temperatures that would otherwise be fierce, but it can also whip up a lively spray on the waves and send plates and glasses crashing to the floor from restaurant tables.

I would always choose June or September for a holiday myself if we didn't already live on the island for much of the year. It is true we wouldn't have to worry about dates that fitted in with school holidays, and that I don't have the same cultural need to congregate with old friends on Assumption Day. This is clearly a very important date in the Orthodox religious calendar and commemorating it, both at the morning church service and the solemn procession around the streets that follows, is one way in which Greeks confirm their identities.

From the first day of August the streets of Chora began to fill up with holidaymakers, many of whom were born on the island and return every year. Since Marylle had a number of friends among them, I spent more time than usual there with her. In the nature of things the main street was something of a fashion parade, of course, with designer clothes of all kinds in evidence during the morning and evening walkabouts.

There couldn't have been a greater contrast when Yorgo and his gang of aged builders turned up at the house in their patched jeans and working shoes early one morning. I don't think Yorgo understood the concept of any other kind of holiday than a national festival, anyway, and they were there to finish paving the terrace as well as doing a number of other jobs for us.

We had been out to a fairly elegant party the night before and he stared at me without expression as I stumbled out in my dressing gown to answer his thunderous knocking at the door.

— Good morning. Had a good night did you? I can see it in your eyes. We'll get started straight away if that's all right then.

It was only just after half past seven in the morning but the vigorous old mason looked so brisk and workmanlike standing there that I began to wake up at once out of shame.

— Of course. I'll be with you when I've shaved myself.

He nodded with a flash of his fierce blue eyes.

— I always do that the evening before. Saves me time in the mornings.

I was working out that the stubborn old man must be seventy by now as I scraped at myself in the mirror and found it hard to credit how much energy he still had. He also had lots of pride and discipline but I had the feeling he was motivated by something more than good habits. I was towelling my face when I remembered a story he had told me once about an elderly relative who had come back from America earlier in the century with savings of about twenty thousand dollars.

This would have been a fortune in Greece in those days and

the relative had lived comfortably from the income he had received after converting it into Greek drachmas. With the advent of the second world war the money lost most of its value, however, and he was left with failing health and almost nothing from his savings.

I felt sure that Yorgo was driven to keep his strength and skills for as long as possible and that he almost certainly preferred land and property to savings accounts.

There seemed to be a row going on between him and Yanni, his sixty year old assistant, when I went out on to the terrace, while the other older workman was busy mixing cement. They had always shouted at each other, but this time Yanni's voice was really loud and it was only when they both laughed delightedly that I realised it had been a friendly exchange but that Yorgo had become a little hard of hearing.

It was the only sign of age he showed as he worked on through the steamy morning, although I was wilting just from typing in my study and going out for an occasional stroll in the garden. When he called for lunch I joined them at an old table out of the sun and accepted the usual offerings from the plastic boxes of food their wives had given them. It was the time for a ritual exchange of views and Yorgo started by asking me what I thought about Greek politicians.

I replied that I didn't know enough about them but was inclined to think that anyone who made a career trying to run other people's lives was suspect in my eyes anyway.

He cackled with harsh laughter at this and launched into an anecdote about some politician I didn't completely understand. When he started one of his usual shouting matches with Yanni I sat there trying to think of what memory they stirred in me. They were certainly both abrasive men who weren't unkind but unlikely to be sympathetic to anyone who lacked their resilience and tremendous capacity for work.

Both were also extremely strong, of course, with chests like tough old barrels hooped with iron, although Yorgo also had an authority about him that was more to do with his obstinate and commanding character. He looked amiable enough sitting there with his bald head and corded neck, but I had seen him in a couple of towering rages and knew that the other two were a little in awe of him.

They were talking about food now and were dismissive of people who ate badly and smoked cigarettes all the time.

— The trouble is that people want to die too quickly these days, said Yorgo decisively. They don't know how to work hard and still live for a long time like my grandfather.

— What did he do?

— He was a mason. I learned my trade from him. He was known all over the island by his nickname which meant the man who looks like a lamp.

— Why did they call him that?

When Yanni laughed at my question the old mason scowled at him before turning back to me.

— Because he was bald, he said shortly. We'll get back to work now.

It was only when they turned up with a young man to help carry sand and stones for them two days later that the memory they had awoken in me came to the surface. The lad was amiable enough but he was not long out of school and clearly found that work interrupted his daydreams, since he stopped when nobody told him what to do and stared vacantly into space. He just looked puzzled when Yanni started deriding most young people over lunch for being lazy and having their heads stuffed full of useless theory.

He was getting into his stride when I suddenly found myself remembering the formidable men on the housing estate where I grew up as a child. Although most of them had been in the armed services at one time, and respected genuine authority, they had also been suspicious of anyone whose claim to command rested only on what they thought of as a formal and empty education. They were men who had often paid the price for the bad judgement of those who professed to be their superiors, and had learned to survive only by trusting people with few words and their own capacity for hard work.

Of course they were convinced they had earned their harsh moral certainty because of the arduous lives they had led and it was clear that Yanni would have agreed with them. He was telling the baffled young man at that moment that there had been no buses on the island in his day and that children from his village who got through to the secondary school at Chora had to walk there.

I worked out that he was talking about a distance of about ten miles and looked across the table at him in astonishment.

— How often did they have to do that?

— Every week. They stayed with a family and walked back every Saturday.

— How long did it take them?

— Three hours there and the same back again.

There had been a high wind since Yorgo and his men had started work but it was really blowing a gale when I took him down a bottle of beer later. He was working on the stone bench and table on the rocky station by the stream and the large plane tree on the other bank was threshing wildly above him. I don't imagine a hurricane could have blown Yorgo anywhere he didn't want to go, however, and I watched him brace himself as he removed the bottle cap with a small flat stone.

— Was it true that some kids had to walk that far to school as a child?

There was a grin that was almost derisive on his leathery face as he wiped the foam from his lips.

— We walked everywhere in those days. I walked to Chora for my violin lessons twice a week when I was twenty.

I ducked as a small leafy branch from the plane tree came flying past my head.

— Who gave you lessons?

— Antonis's uncle.

— Do you still play?

He shook his head as he bent from the waist with a grunt to pick up the branch from the ground.

— Only now and again. Do you have to get up in the night because of your prostate gland?

I stared at him as he snapped some hairy fruit from the piece of foliage.

— Sometimes.

He handed me the fruit as though he was offering me some morsels from his lunch box.

— What you do is boil these in water and drink a glass of the liquid every morning. It works I can tell you.

As I walked back up the path I was thinking that there was nothing extraordinary in a man like Yorgo knowing that sort of thing and having walked over forty miles every week to learn the violin. Every man can be surprising, and I have never met anyone who wasn't creative in some way, even if they didn't like to talk about it, but it seemed years since I had known someone quite so resolute and sensitive at the same time. I suppose that what I was really feeling was heartened by knowing a man of his age with so much eagerness and stamina still in him and I found myself running up the steps in a little burst of animal spirits.

It was more windy if anything the following day, with everything in the valley in a great thick swirl of branches and leaves, although it was still as hot as I have known it on the island. There was some further work on the terrace to be done, as well as the building of the patio down by the mill, but Yorgo was demanded elsewhere and it was two weeks before he turned up again.

In the meantime the wind died to a caressing breeze, the sea looked like beautiful green jelly, and I caught up with the swimming I hadn't done in the previous couple of weeks.

The night before Yorgo's old stagers were due back we went

Marylle and I at the stone table above the stream

to a party held on a jetty under the stars with several white yachts moored at the other side of the harbour. A couple of guitars were produced at midnight and I sat listening to people sing about their country as though they were sitting around a camp fire that last burned high when Alexander the Great was alive.

I must have looked wild and haggard again when I let Yorgo in early in the morning but he said nothing and carefully started work down near the mill so we wouldn't hear too much noise. It had been a beautiful few days and at lunch Yanni chatted away cheerfully about having walked for a couple of hours on the Sunday to fish from the rocks at the tip of the island.

As he knotted the cloth around his lunch box Yorgo hummed away to himself and then told Marylle that he wanted us to visit him at his village the following Monday during a local religious festival.

— I want you to see something, he said. It's a friend of mine who's done up this old house in a way I know you'll love.

He nodded at us in his own emphatic way.

— It's good to see people wanting to do things in the old style.

A couple of evenings later we took a visiting friend out for an early meal at the hill taverna above our village with the small tribe of kids. It was almost at the end of August and the mountain opposite seemed to glow from inside with a strange orange light of its own. There was a melting silver sea in the distance and the sky was slowly changing to a pinkish colour where it wasn't discoloured by a mist of heat.

It had been a beautiful summer and it suddenly occurred to me that I had only been to the cinema under the stars twice since it had opened its doors three months earlier.

CHAPTER SIXTEEN

$\mathscr{I}$T HAD BEEN SIXTEEN MONTHS SINCE YORGO AND HIS ancient crew of former mariners had first arrived to start building a roof over the room with the giant fireplace. They had only worked a few short stretches of about ten days each since then, whenever we had the money to pay them, but the top level of the house, including its handsome terrace, was ready for inspection by anybody now.

Any doubts we might have had once about whether we had bought wisely had long since melted into a huge warm satisfaction with the house and its position in the valley. After all, we had lived in it for most of the time, and it had already changed our lives in many green and subtle ways.

We planned to call in Yorgo again to work on the rooms down on the lower level, where the animals had been kept, but that would have to wait a while. Already, we knew that we had at least one more room there than we thought. Yorgo had pushed a stick through a gap in a stone wall of the room where the cow had once been tied and discovered an empty space behind it.

One of his last jobs for us had been to pave the terrace, and we had asked Leonidas, the electrician, to lay a cable across it first so that we could fix a lantern on the wall above the garden. Since the warm evenings were drawing in earlier now we had started to switch it on quite early and the glow could be seen like a pale yellow flame between the trees from the road above the valley.

Marylle was sitting out on the terrace in a striped deck chair when I came down the steps one August evening and I saw a falling star, or some screaming astral debris, hurtle down the sky behind her. She was reading something and didn't notice it but it looked to me as though the entire universe was about to put on a show for her.

The house itself needed another coat of whitewash after all the work but it also glowed nicely in the shadows and we only needed to start thinking about the kind of furniture it deserved. Marylle had bought some lace island curtains for the windows and I was hoping to find a solid old desk to type on instead of the rickety green table I had been using until then.

Most of the villagers seemed to know that I was writing about life among them by now and were usually happy to pass on scraps of information they thought might interest me.

I was in the café bar one morning with a little wooden frame I had found in the lower level of the house, which had obviously been used as a door for the chicken coup. It had catches of some very hard wood and I was going to get the carpenter to clean it up for me and use it as a heavy frame for a photograph.

The old man with the walnut face who lived further down the valley was there and he wandered across to inspect it after a while.

— Where did you find this?

When I told him he nodded sagely and fingered a catch on it shaped like a thick wooden tongue.

— My father used to carve things like this. It's made from a mulberry tree.

— I was wondering what wood it was.

He moved the catch to and fro.

— It's one of the toughest woods there is. They used to cut it in January under a full moon.

I've no idea whether he was pulling my leg or not, and another villager I spoke to later said he probably was, but then people from the same area usually make a habit of disagreeing with each other about their customs and traditions, whichever country they're from.

I knew there was a religious festival coming up shortly to celebrate some miraculous event at the village church and it was difficult enough to find out what this was all about. I was told that there is a festival held in all churches dedicated to the Virgin Mary on the date in question but the villagers seem to believe that it also commemorates something special to the church which happened long ago.

When I asked Nico about it he said there had been two urns in the church one evening with only a little oil in them but the following morning they had been discovered to be full.

Papa Andreas shook his head when I asked whether this was true and launched into what legend in the village declares to be the history of the church. He confirmed what a nineteenth century priest had told James Bent, that it was built on what had been a temple to Dionysos, but had been an Orthodox church for over fourteen hundred years.

— In the old days it was a custom to drink a cup of the water that runs through the church after every mass, he went on, but one Sunday in the seventh century there wasn't enough to fill the last person's cup.

He rose to his feet to greet an old couple I hadn't seen before and smiled when he sat down again.

— Of course, everyone thought the spring water had dried up but it is said that it started flowing again after the priest had prayed and that's what we celebrate every year.

When the day itself arrived there were more cars near the

church and along past the café bar than I had ever seen before at that time in the morning. The church bells had been tolling emphatically since half past seven and there were a number of people I recognised from other villages among the crowds filing into the church.

It was obviously an important festival because there was another older priest officiating with Papa Andreas and three more chanters than usual. One of them was the husband of Antonis's sister, who I had seen working in the garden a couple of times after arriving from Athens with his very sick wife. Apparently, he had been a chanter in Constantinople when younger, and it seemed to me that he sang, not only with beautiful control, but also with a kind of sad, almost oriental howl in his voice.

The café bar was full of people from all over the area and it was only when Papa Andreas turned up in his handsome robes that I learned why there were so many. It seemed that the villages further down the valley used to take water from the spring for their crops and the miracle in the church which restored it has been celebrated to this day.

There was to be music and dancing that evening but I knew that Antonis wouldn't be playing the violin this year. He still scarcely ventured from his house, although I had seen him a couple of times wandering like a lost silver ghost in the road outside when driving up to one of the hill tavernas.

Sitting outside on the terrace that afternoon I noticed only two hawks circling sternly above the trees, so, presumably, their fledglings had departed to find their own territories elsewhere on the island.

It was almost nine o'clock when we walked up the steps to the café bar and I heard the husband of Antonis's sister chanting softly to her as we passed their house. We saw Hariklia waving to us frantically as we came opposite her house and she came trotting around the corner a few minutes later to ask if she could join our table for the festivities.

She turned up twenty minutes later wearing her best frock but used our table only as a base, from which she kept darting away to talk to other ladies. It was clearly important for her to be seen to be in a party, but she was primarily interested in keeping up with the local gossip and seeing what was going on.

There was a very lively and expressive violinist with the group of musicians, who I learned were from Vourkoti, and it wasn't long before some ladies began dancing with stately dipping movements, handkerchiefs held neatly between them, like a line of respectable swans.

When we left, Hariklia was standing at another table watching the dancers with hands held together and a faraway look on her face.

The following morning she called to me across the water and, when I went up to her house to find out what she wanted, I was presented with a large bag of purslane, nine brown eggs and a beaming heap of fresh tomatoes.

It was almost September now, and the sky was a high glazed blue most of the time, although it could look threatening early some mornings and the occasional wind still shook the crowded trees. When Marylle had to go to Athens for a few days I busied myself in the garden, or just sat at our new stone table above the sloping rocks staring into the stream.

A few years earlier I had been seriously ill, but felt now that I could almost live for ever in this green and healthy valley. The weather could be wild sometimes, of course, with storms lashing the island in winter, and even snowfalls, but the valley always lay folded nicely between the high terraces on either side, full of trees and promise.

This sense of richness came from the clear fact that it had been domesticated to some extent over the centuries but not controlled in any rigorous way. Although many of its former inhabitants had left, and none of the water mills functioned any longer, it was still obvious that it had been worked on by people who had themselves been organically involved with the valley.

The stone walls which supported the ascending terraces showed how much labour they had put into it, but there were few other signs that they had ever tried to interfere with its natural character.

As far as Marylle and I were concerned, they had left a small paradise behind, in which we could live from the land if necessary, and which was also full of its own extraordinary life.

I knew that my own sense of personal renewal had come about because of all these plaited and singing reasons. The energy around us enchanted me as much as the springs that fed the stream running through the valley, not to mention the waterfall bouncing away outside my study window all through the year.

At the same time we were lucky to be living there with the kind of characters who sometimes make me think that Greece should be declared an international park for the preservation of valuable human archetypes. It wasn't difficult to imagine a whole lineage of busy-fingered women stretching away behind Hariklia, grubbing up the roots and herbs of the earth and cherishing precious seeds through the winter. It was certainly impossible to think of anyone more deft and ingenious with his hands than Antonis, even though he was wary in the extreme as a person and always liable to bouts of serious pessimism.

The quality I admired most in the characters we knew was their practical versatility in face of the daily challenges of living in the valley. Since they all wore their flaws and virtues on their sleeves, I began to think that this ability to respond variously to life was what made a human being and that it was alien to become specialised in one activity. After a while the people we met from the world of affairs, whether they were croupiers or bank managers, stock brokers or book keepers, seemed to be mostly just functions of the system that defined them, with little authentic personal life of their own.

I'm pretty sure it was this recognition of how human the people around us were that had helped me start feeling more alive in myself again. Most of the people I had known before had seemed to owe more of themselves to emotional problems in their childhood and social possibilities than to whatever it is that makes us tick as creatures of the earth. They had been shaped by a sophisticated culture which sustained them by remote control, but their relationships with each other and the world of nature were confused most of the time. The result was that their problems were largely psychological and they weren't at all certain of what it meant to be human.

The people from the valley were in no doubt that they were here on earth to bear witness to the miracle of life itself and go to church every week. It was a small community full of the extraordinary facts of daily existence and there was still a sense of astonishment about what happened regularly around them. At the same time they took it for granted that each person had their own character and that this explained why everyone responded to emotional problems in different ways. Since I had grown tired of metropolitan behaviour I was happy to be where reality started in the earth and people had characters rather than behavioural difficulties.

I was clear in my mind that the two characters who had done most for me were Nico and old Yorgo, the mason, although it is true I had never seen either of them handling emotional situations. Of course Yorgo wasn't from our village but he got on famously with Nico while working for us and it was obvious they had a lot in common. I don't think they ever considered putting chemicals on the food they grew for themselves and I never saw either of them push away their plate without a grunt of relish and intense personal satisfaction.

They both thrived on keeping themselves busy also and I couldn't imagine them complaining about any work they had to do. Whether they were digging trenches, carting rocks, or tilling the earth, I always had the feeling they were fuelling some core of pride deep inside themselves at the same time. I also came to understand that their tremendous energy came from a fierce need for independence and an appetite for life both had to an almost outrageous degree.

I had benefited a great deal from the simplicity of life in the village and the pleasure most people seemed to take in small matters. What I had learned from Nico and Yorgo was the remarkably simple truth that the best way to feel real is to work hard and live as naturally as possible.

One still hot morning in the third week of September Marylle and I drove up to the old ruined house in the hills behind the village where I was to help Nico tread his grapes. I was under the impression that he had broken the rules and given Marylle special dispensation to attend this male rite, but we found his wife and mother-in-law there as well. It appeared he didn't mind women being present so long as they didn't actually crush the grapes, which was fine by me because we were served steaming hot coffee and little pastries with walnuts and honey almost as soon as we arrived.

It was the first time we had been to the place where Nico kept the fodder for his animals and, as we walked up a broken path to the house, there was a dirty white mule's skull propped on a stick to one side of it. There was also a wooden cross nailed above the open door, and a bunch of garlic hanging from under the eaves, all there to protect against the ubiquitous evil eye.

Nico himself showed us around the place, which was on two levels, with most of the downstairs area a largish byre where his cows were fed and watered. Upstairs there was an iron bed in one room, with a dusty still resting on its grey blanket and a large glass flagon of raki on the floor. There were bales of hay and barley in a storeroom next to it and, outside on a flat terrace, a great rough carpet of blue and black grapes drying in the sun.

The concrete trough in which the grapes were to be crushed was on the ground below, but what caught the eye at once was a great bulky sack of a cow tethered to a post in the smallest farmyard I have ever seen. I could see two other swollen animals on the narrow terrace of land above where we were standing and, as they shook their heads mournfully, there came the most profound baritone roar from somewhere.

Looking around for the animal which had made this astonishing sound, we saw a young coffee and cream calf in a small pen lift its silken head and bellow again.

Marylle made appropriate female noises of sweet astonishment and Nico grinned at her before jumping down to the ground beside the trough.

— There's a new baby calf up there, he said, nodding to where the two cows up on the higher ground were still swinging their enormous heads. We've got time to take a look at it if you don't mind getting a bit dirty.

We had to pass through the pen to get up to the next level of land and the beautiful young calf with the extraordinary lungs backed away against an earthen wall in alarm. It had great slanting olive eyes, skin that looked as though it belonged on some exotic fruit, and tall elegantly split hooves on which it teetered like a young girl on her first pair of platform shoes.

When we had scrambled up we saw that one cow was looking exhausted as it swayed heavily in front of us, while the other, which was extraordinarily pregnant, was tied to an old olive tree. On the ground between them lay the baby calf with its front legs daintily crossed and nostrils bubbling a little.

It looked asleep at first but then lifted its head towards us with weary blinking eyes and Nico stooped at once to kiss it on the face.

— It was only born three hours ago, he said with one of his mad happy smiles. I was up here to make sure there weren't any problems.

As he stood up the pregnant cow bawled at him and

Marylle looked across nervously as it strained on the rope.

— What's the matter with her?

— She wants to adopt the little one, Nico said. That's why I had to tie her up.

He was humming cheerfully to himself as we clambered back down to where his son Yanni was washing a pair of wellington boots with great care. After pulling them on he climbed into the trough as Nico started shovelling down the grapes from the terrace above. There was a hole in one side of the trough and a clean empty drum beneath it with a sieved funnel to take the grape juice.

The hole in the trough also had a small thick sheaf of fennel jammed into it which I discovered later was there to catch any pips and bits of skin getting into the funnel.

As the grapes tumbled around him Yianni just trod solemnly up and down like a sentry on duty while the muddy brown juice from them trickled down through the funnel and into the drum. The trickle turned into a stream and, while Nico was taking away the drum to empty it into a much larger one in the byre, Yanni climbed out of the trough to remove his wellington boots and socks. I stood there carefully observing the rocking motion of his bare feet on the grapes after he had hopped in again and, finally, Nico and I climbed over the sides to join him.

We linked arms as we danced together and Nico turned every so often to yell across to his son as he bobbed up and down beside me on the mashed and bleeding grapes.

— Watch me. This is the way you do it.

Every time he heard these hectic commands a broad flashing grin crossed Yanni's face and I realised that father and son were playing a game with each other. Yanni was an intelligent boy but I guessed that he considered the education he had received at school to be no more than a useful guide to the ways of the larger world. He had learned the more important lessons about work and life from his father, who clearly

Yanni, myself and Nico treading the grapes

regarded it as a sacred male duty to pass down what he knew to his sons. I had been roped in on several occasions to confirm the general likelihood of some sexual experience Nico had been describing, and each time Yanni had listened with proper gravity and attention.

He was obviously expert at pressing grapes but didn't mind that his father was pretending to treat him as a novice and nudged me delightedly when the shout came again:

— This is how you do it.

It was ten minutes later when we stopped for Nico to empty the drum and then to sit down for some tender apple pie made by Nico's quiet little mother-in-law and glasses of raki. I had estimated that there had been about eighteen inches of grapes on the floor of the trough but understood that treading them properly was serious work and that I had probably been in the way. I stayed in the background this time when Nico's father-in-law appeared and helped Yanni carry on with the job.

Another five drums were emptied during the next couple of hours and I was interested to see the procedure they used to extract the last of the juice. First of all they pushed the remaining jellied mass to one side of the trough and Yanni braced himself with his hands on the ledge behind him to push it against the wall with his bare feet. This created pressure from one direction and, with his spritely grandfather treading down firmly from above, more juice was squeezed out than I would have thought possible.

There was more to come, however, and this was released by placing flat heavy stones on top of the grape debris and then standing on them. The final trick was to punch holes with a broom stick handle into what was now just damp sludge until the last drops of fluid oozed out on to the floor of the trough.

This was swept out through the hole and the ceremonial treading of the season's grapes was over. We were to take delivery of the hundred litres of must we had ordered later in the day when Nico could bring it down to the house with his mules.

I stood there in the sun talking to his wife and mother-in-law while he was busy somewhere. They were sitting on the ground under a mulberry tree collecting fallen fruit which would be used later to make another strong spirit. The broad fertile valley leading down to the sea below was heavy with thick light and there was no sign of life in it anywhere that I could see.

A pile of dry cow dung with about a dozen walnuts on top was piled near the tree and a lone skeletal dragonfly skimmed crazily over the heads of the two women.

When I walked into the house I found Nico measuring the alcoholic strength of the must with a hydrometer. There was a satisfied look on his face as he took it out of the great drum.

— Sixteen degrees, he said. Stronger than it was last year.

I watched as he filled a number of goat skins with the must and laid them gently by the open door. He spilt a little but was in a hurry now and went out to fetch the bulky cow down by the pen and its noisy calf before we left. The cow submitted without protest to being tethered to the trough but the calf bellowed hugely as its nice cloven hooves skittered precariously on the wet stone floor.

We had bought a barrel for the wine a week earlier from Nico's brother Leonidas, who had also constructed a simple platform from two poles for it in the little stone building where the mill was housed. Apparently, it was one of several barrels with a capacity of a hundred litres which he had bought for his own use some eighteen years before.

Although he didn't make his own wine nowadays, the barrel had already been used several times and didn't need rinsing with water. He was insistent that I poured a litre of rough brandy into it, however, which I understood was for disinfecting as well as giving the wine more body.

14 ROBERT LEIGH, *Sunlight in the wine*

The problem was that he had given me instructions to slosh the brandy around inside the barrel once a day and the only way I could do this was by lifting it up around the middle and jiggle up and down. It was the only time in my life I have been able to appreciate how an extremely pregnant woman must feel when walking down a hill.

It was late afternoon when Nico finally showed up with his mules and the bloated and shining goat skins. After shaking the barrel vigorously once more, he inserted the wide sieved funnel into its neck and began pouring out the must. The way he accomplished this was by lifting each full goat skin on to his right shoulder and then dipping down to direct the heavy brown flow into the funnel.

The next step was to remove the patch of wood in the neck of the barrel and cover the opening with a material which would allow the must to breathe but keep out midges and other insects. A couple of months earlier we had been presented with a tiny silver cross and some almond sweets wrapped in a piece of muslin at a wedding reception. I had intended keeping the cross and the hard little sweets for my mother but knew she wouldn't mind if I used the muslin to protect our new wine.

When I weighted down the scrap of delicate white material on top of the barrel with heavy stones, it lay there like a trapped lace handkerchief and Nico was tickled pink.

— The wine is sure to taste sweeter now, he said. Don't forget to buy the gypsum before the end of next week.

He had already explained to me that we would have to replace the patch of wood in the barrel's neck after ten days and caulk it firmly to stop air getting in. The wine itself would be ready for drinking after another thirty days in theory, although there were different ideas about this and, in any event, it depended on weather conditions. There was apparently one thirsty priest in another village who insisted that only daylight hours were meant, so that he could halve the time and drink his wine earlier, and we knew that Yorgo up at Vourkoti didn't open his barrels until the following Spring.

When Marylle and I ate up at the café bar that evening it seemed that most of the villagers knew about our venture into wine making and had their own suggestions about what we should do. I was surprised when several thought we ought to have put a chemical yeast in with the must and one man even recommended stacking charcoal around the bottom of the barrel, although nobody else could see the point of this.

After hearing everybody out, we decided that Nico was right and that we should let the wine develop naturally, but did take the advice of one neighbour to remove the onions I had stored in the mill house. It hadn't occurred to me that their smell might corrupt the must, and I certainly didn't want this to happen, particularly since I love roast onions with a simple earthy wine.

After I had taken down the onions from the beams where I had hung them the following morning, I listened at the open neck of the barrel and heard a low drunken muttering. It had become more argumentative by the afternoon and the next morning it sounded as though a million bubbles were having a wicked party. The thought occurred to me as I closed the mill door behind me that life itself might even be the result of some chemical change taking place in the universe which was causing effervescence here on earth.

I slept only fitfully the next couple of nights and was tempted to pad down in the darkness to check whether the barrel was still buzzing. The sounds of marvellous agitation did begin to die away the following week but Nico assured me that this was normal.

When he turned up to seal the neck of the barrel I felt almost as though I was present at a medical emergency. I came back at least a couple of times after he had gone to stare at the barrel, but it just lay there mute and bandaged on its poles and I had no idea whether the wine inside was living or not.

There was digging to do in the garden but I found myself just lazing around a lot of the time over the next few weeks. I was enjoying the solemn peace of late autumn now that the house could be lived in without having to sweep out great piles of dust every morning.

We hadn't succeeded in doing everything we had planned over the past eighteen months and I was still hoping that Antonis would recover enough to get the mill working for us some time. It was also a pity that Marylle hadn't been able to make the festival happen but she was hopeful that Bambi Ballard would pop up again from wherever she had been dancing and they could start to put it together again.

It hadn't rained in months and pretty well the whole of Greece was parched, although nobody seriously expected the drought to last as long as it had the previous year. The weather continued hot and sweltering until early November, however, but then Greece isn't a country where the expected happens often and the Greeks themselves have almost made unpredictability into a national virtue.

I should have been used to them by now but I still finished up exasperated beyond measure sometimes by what I saw as a lack of reason and proportion in the way they talked about things. On the other hand, I had lived in England long enough to know that what is called rational language there reflects more of a desire for order than anything else and often makes people strangers to each other.

Although the Greeks invented democracy, which was the first kind of society not based exclusively on kinship ties, most of the people I know all seem to have about fifty cousins and give the impression they are on shouting terms with everybody else. It is certainly true that almost all of them would prefer to work for a cousin, however shifty, than for some efficient but impersonal organisation run by distant accountants, which is presumably why many people in the larger European shopping mall despair of them.

We read that the water shortage in Athens was so acute that churches across the country were holding special services to pray for rain. There was a danger that dust collecting on electricity cables might cause a blackout and, in fact, this did happen for several hours one day. It was certainly not the weather for opening our barrel of wine, and Nico said we probably ought to wait another couple of weeks when he came around with cheese and eggs, but also suggested we might try a glass of it between us that morning.

The liquid that came out when I turned the tap on cautiously was reddish and very cloudy but it was indisputably wine. There was a nice vinous breath on it and it had more of a kick than I had expected when I drank a little. Nico was delighted with both its colour and strength and waxed almost lyrically about what a superb vintage it was going to be.

— We'll have enough good wine to last us all through the winter, he said. All we need now is some walnuts with honey and logs to keep the fires burning.

It was another week before we got some rain, but it was only a thin drizzle, and we had to wait several days more before some low clouds finally collapsed over the island. The downpour only lasted a couple of hours, however, and then the sun came out again as though it had only been intended as a joke. We hadn't seen Nico in some time but I wanted to take advantage of the weather to try our wine again and decided not to wait for him.

When I brought some up in a carafe we saw that it had turned a pleasant rusty colour but certainly looked clear now. The sun went behind a small cloud as I poured two glasses but then came out again and I looked up to see a movement high up on a terrace below a house with bougainvillaea still glowing on its wall.

A moment later a white mule came into view and Nico lifted an arm in salute as he looked down and saw me raise my glass to him. I couldn't hear him, of course, but had a fancy that he shouted to me before disappearing behind two cypress trees.

— That's the way you do it.

Marylle and I sat there drinking wine slowly in the late sunlight while I tried to work out whether I liked it or not. I thought it tasted of something damp and woody, but this was the smell down in the mill house and was probably what my mouth was expecting. There was also a strange medicinal hint to it, which I wasn't certain about at all at first, but then after the second glass, decided it helped give the wine a marvellously robust and healthy flavour.

It was quite different to any wine from Nico's grapes I had drunk before, but that is the beginning of true pleasure to me, when things happen as they always have in life, but in a way that seems completely unexpected each time.

*

'SUNLIGHT IN THE WINE'
BY
ROBERT LEIGH

THIS BOOK WAS PRODUCED IN GREECE BY GEORGE
DARDANOS AND CHRISTOS STAVROPOULOS UNDER
THE IMPRINT TYPOTHITO. THE COVER WAS
DESIGNED BY KIRIAKOS ATHANASIADES AND THE
TEXT PROOF READ BY ATHANASIA SAKELLARIOU.
FIRST PUBLISHED JUNE 1996.